The Art of G. K. Chesterton

The Art of G. K. Chesterton

Alzina Stone Dale

 Loyola University Press/Chicago

Loyola University Press
3441 North Ashland Avenue
Chicago, Illinois 60657

Design by C. L. Tornatore

Library of Congress Cataloging in Publication Data

Dale, Alzina Stone, 1931-
    The art of G. K. Chesterton.

    Includes index.
    1. Chesterton, G. K. (Gilbert Keith), 1874-1936.
2. Authors, English—20th century—Biography. I. Title.
PR4453.C4Z5878   1985   828'.91209|B| 85-18165
ISBN 0-8294-0516-X

To
Serena Spencer
in whose library I first met
"The Man Who Was Chesterton"

Contents

Preface

G. K. Chesterton, The Invisible Man

In 1983 some Chesterton chalk drawings were offered for sale in Sotheby's New York catalogue. When Dr. Lyle Dorsett, Curator of the Wade Collection at Wheaton College, Wheaton, Illinois, saw them, he felt they would make an important addition to the Wade's Chesterton archives which already included some G.K.C. drawings and sketches that had belonged to Chesterton's bibliographer, John Sullivan. Dr. Dorsett talked about the drawings to Father Daniel Flaherty, S.J., Director of Loyola University Press in Chicago. The Press, which had plans to celebrate the 50th anniversary of G. K. Chesterton's death in 1986 by re-issuing some of his work, offered to purchase the drawings and donate them to the Wade Collection, provided they might in turn be used as illustrations for a book re-introducing Chesterton to the late 20th Century. The idea for this book was born.

Next I was asked if I would like to write the text which would accompany these Chesterton drawings and sketches, with the aim of giving the reader a refresher course in G.K.C., in order to reintroduce him to the contemporary world. When Gilbert Keith Chesterton died in 1936, the whole world mourned his passing; fifty years later, apart from his Father Brown mysteries and an occasional quotation by a public figure, very few people can answer the question, "Who was G.K.C.?" He has become one of his own invisible men, left out of the textbooks altogether or mentioned only as a friend of others like G. B. Shaw or H. G. Wells or Max Beerbohm.

G. K. Chesterton's convictions about the human condition, however, expressed in his inimitable way—like his comment that "for a landlady considering a lodger, it is important to know his income, but still more important to know his philosophy" —have a lot to say to our Age of Anxiety, which is not so very different from his own time. Religion itself has proved to be far from dead, but our warring extremists of every description cry out for the very qualities Chesterton personified and defended: reason and common sense. His work is not only wise and witty, literature in the best meaning of that term, but it also makes fascinating and compelling reading, because Chesterton singlehandedly undertook to defend Western Civilization with his own brand of flair and imagination. In doing so, he also demonstrated that his roots were not reactionary but truly radical, for, as he said, "real development is not leaving things behind, as on a road, but drawing life from them as from a root."

In this book, featuring some newly discovered art by Chesterton, it is also appropriate to consider him as an artist, who habitually used both visual and verbal art forms. During his lifetime G.K.C. called all craftsmen "artists," while he always insisted that he himself was only "a jolly journalist," dealing with ephemeral things, not a man of letters creating great masterpieces. But physically and spiritually, Chesterton should be portrayed "in the

round" as an engaging man of many talents who refused to take himself seriously—but always took his ideas very seriously indeed. He needs to be seen again as an articulate artist who turned his draftsmen's eye on the world to help his fellow men "exercise the eye until it learns to see the startling facts that run across the landscape as plain as a painted fence," as much as the kindly giant who doodled through business meetings, illuminated all his texts, and carried chalks in his pocket when he went visiting children.

The main purpose of this book is to re-draw his portrait by coloring in once more the large, blank outline of his portly and gallant figure. Wearing his brigand's costume of flowing cape and slouched hat, armed with his beloved swordstick, Chesterton must become visible again, standing ready in his fencer's pose to face up to his friends like Shaw with whom he debated the crucial issues of his time and ours.

The case for Chesterton in 1986 can rest upon an observation which he made about Geoffrey Chaucer, another writer often dismissed as belonging to "the good old days." Chesterton said that

when corruption and chaos are disturbing ordinary minds, and many good men are only worried and serious, it has often happened that a great man could apparently be frivolous and appear in history . . . as a great buffoon. . . . These rare and sane spirits . . . |appear in| a revolutionary epoch or a dissolving civilization. And there is always something about them puzzling to those who see their frivolity from the outside and not their faith from the inside . . . [for] their faith is not a stagnation but an equilibrium.

This statement is yet another version of his more famous statement that "we have to find a way to contrive to be at once astonished at the world and yet at home in it."

His critics have seen Chesterton as a romantic and childlike giant, a jolly journalist filled with gusto who created tremendous trifles, or the uncritical, optimistic Christian who either is hiding a deep despair or too naive to worry. They misunderstood his use of paradox as a way of holding warring truths in tension, or "combining furious opposites by keeping them both and keeping them both furious," just as they fail to recognize his deliberate lifelong search for sanity and common sense. Most of all they ignore the fact that he, too, was born in our modern world, which he called the "twilight of a great post-revolutionary epoch," in which Western man was living off his Christian capital.

In literary terms, Chesterton has been hard to categorize and easy to ignore, because he did not work seriously in the "right forms" like the realistic novels of an Arnold Bennett or a John Galsworthy. Instead, he practiced his trade on whatever assignments came his way and flourished in every branch of literature from poetry to biography, becoming a "master without a masterpiece" but, paradoxically, author of half a dozen "minor masterpieces" still in print. His artistic aim was to make it look easy, and he genuinely envied Chaucer's good fortune of writing at a time when he could write for everybody, the intellectuals and the ordinary people, and be understood and appreciated by both.

In spiritual terms, the late 20th century has more in common with its beginning than it once thought. Religion itself has not proved to be a stage that mankind has progressed beyond, and it is no longer "reactionary" to recognize, as Chesterton did, that the world is a moral battlefield. We know that we live in a universe of anarchy and negation where only those with faith can preserve the moral energy civilization needs to survive, while time itself has shown that Chesterton asked the right questions of the future, which he said could only be seen "mirrored in the shining shield of the past."

Among many causes upon which he took positions unfashionable in his day, and that have come alive in our own, he stood four square behind a belief in the literary genius of Charles Dickens, the maintenance of an English political party of the center, and he stood against elitism, cronyism, and Establishment Old Boys' networks. He believed in a "Little England" nation-state, not the British Raj; in the rights of the displaced Palestinians in a Jewish Homeland; and, in Distributism, stood for the whole concept of "small is beautiful" against rampant industrialism and ecological disaster. He fought for the widespread ownership of property, as the sole means of keeping men free, and against eugenics, social engineering, and the benevolent dictatorship of a Socialist Welfare State.

Most appropriately for our post-1985 world, Chesterton challenged (and feared) the power of the media—of which he was also proud to be a working member— asking "Who guards the guardians?" Most important to him, who grew up in a modern, intellectual, and agnostic culture, he became a convinced orthodox Christian through the arguments of its despisers. He then defended "Christendom" as the true source for Western Civilization's values, believing that the Incarnation and the Fall were the justification for the democratic rights of men.

G. K. Chesterton is a man for the ages, and our age needs to hear his jovial voice again, engaged with a chuckle in reducing arguments to absurdity or turning them upside down, in order to keep us from tearing down the lamppost so that "what we might have discussed under the . . . lamp, we now must discuss in the dark."

This book will first describe Chesterton's life, then offer some observations about him as the artist at work. Just as many of his apt remarks will be quoted in the text to give the flavor of the man, so, scattered throughout the volume, the reader will find examples of Chesterton's art, including the set of his chalk drawings done in pastels upon ordinary brown paper which were auctioned by Sotheby's, samples of his notebook doodling, his book illustrations and his cartoons.

Preface

I should like to take this opportunity to thank the people who helped me with this book:

Dr. Lyle Dorsett and the Wade Collection Staff

Anselmo Carini, Curator of Prints and Drawings,
    The Art Institute of Chicago

Richard Born, Curator of the David and Alfred Smart Gallery,
    University of Chicago

Elizabeth Silvers Conger, MFA

Damaris Hendry Day

My husband, Charles Herrick Dale

ALZINA STONE DALE

The Man Who Was Chesterton

The Toy Theatre: 1874 — 1880

Gilbert Keith Chesterton was born on May 29, 1874, the second child but oldest son of Edward and Mary Louise Chesterton. His parents were both born and bred Londoners who belonged to England's prosperous urban middle class. The Chesterton family had been Londoners for four generations, running their own real estate agency, having begun as agents for an aristocratic family in the western suburb of Kensington. Each generation had prospered and moved up the social and economic scale, just as London itself had become the thriving center of the British Empire. Yet the family was always proudly loyal to Kensington itself, much like Kensington's most illustrious citizen, Queen Victoria, who granted it a coat of arms in her will.

In the prosperous 1870s, when Gilbert Chesterton was born, educated Englishmen like his parents believed that hard work, common sense, scientific technology, and universal education would create worldwide peace and prosperity. The Chestertons were also ardent "Little England" Liberals, who believed in a free trading world of nation-states promoting the rights of the individual. Yet 1875 proved to be a watershed year, when the old European balance of power disappeared under the pressure of the newly created German Empire.

In wealthy Victorian England, however,

where the Liberal Gladstone and the Conservative Disraeli alternated as Prime Minister, there was still a broadbased political consensus but England was under increasing economic strain. The result, as Chesterton said in his *Autobiography*, "was the very reverse of solid [Victorian] respectability . . . its ethics and theology were wearing thin." What he called the Victorian Compromise was breaking up, so that into the late Victorian world there burst "two positive movements . . . the first was Bernard Shaw and the Socialists; the second was Rudyard Kipling and the Imperialists." Chesterton was to resist both in the name of the "orthodox" values of Western Civilization, or "Christendom."

Chesterton grew up in a very cultivated environment, for his parents, especially his father, Edward Chesterton, had a special feeling for literature and all beautiful things. He could just barely remember his grandfather Chesterton, a bearded patriarch who took his small grandson on Sunday walks with another old friend who carried a Prayer Book but never went to church. His mother's family, the Grosjeans, were originally Swiss and Scottish, but by now were thoroughly Anglicized except for their smaller stature, darker coloring, and the tough fighting spirit of which Chesterton's brother Cecil was to be a good example. Their Grosjean grandfather had been a Nonconformist Methodist lay minister and a teetotaler of strong convictions.

Chesterton's own parents were Liberals, both in politics and religion. Tolerant and undogmatic about creeds, they assumed that certain values were self-evident, like the fatherhood of God and the brotherhood of man—but Chesterton said they asked their children to "worship the hearth without the altar."

When Gilbert was born, his parents and his five-year-old sister Beatrice were living in Sheffield Terrace in Kensington. Their house stood on a hill just below the great waterworks on Campden Hill, which he used as the symbol of local patriotism in *The Napoleon of Notting Hill*. He was baptized in the local parish church with the names of Tom Gilbert, his father's cousin, and Keith, the Scottish surname of his maternal grandmother.

Towards the end of his life when he wrote his autobiography, Chesterton's memories themselves demonstrated how vividly he thought in pictures. His very first recollection of the primal happiness of childhood was of a young man with a curly moustache, wearing a crown and carrying a large key of shining yellow, who was walking across a bridge towards a castle where a lady was locked up. It was a scene being played in his father's toy theatre with cardboard puppets. The charm of the toy theatre lay in its positive outlines, with clumps of vegetation and clouds as stiff as bolsters, and he ever after loved frames and limits because they reminded him of the main principle of art, that "it consists of limitations."

The toy theatre shaped Chesterton's artistic imagination the rest of his life, not, as his brother suggested, because it represented a romantic escape from reality, but because the theatre and its magician creator, his father, had shaped his image of God the creator. In his *Autobiography* Chesterton first called his father by the titles he later learned to use for the head of the Church: Pontifex, or Builder of Bridges, and Clavigor, or Key Bearer, he who unlocks the secret of existence.

His next memories were of the sparkling, morning world of childhood, where a white light shone over everything; inside the nursery, as his father painted a white hobby horse, and outside standing on their doorstep with his nurse and sister gazing out over London. These memories all became his primeval past, however, for when he was three, Beatrice Chesterton died. His baby grief was aggravated by the irrational behavior of his father, who turned his daughter's picture to the wall, got rid of all her possessions, and until the day of his death refused to allow anyone to talk of her again. The result was a great crack across Chesterton's world, which he described in *Orthodoxy* by saying that "happiness is bright like the diamond, but as brittle as the windowpane . . . and . . . I was afraid that God would drop the cosmos with a crash."

Two years later, in 1879, the world was redeemed for Gilbert with a fairy tale solution when his brother Cecil was born. No doubt the family had hoped for another girl, but Cecil quickly became the idol of them all, fearless and foolhardy, argumentative and adored. It was really Cecil Chesterton who had the "happiest childhood in literature," for the sight of Cecil choking would send Gilbert screaming

from the room in terror, and all his life his love for his brother would help to determine Chesterton's career.

Shortly after Cecil's birth, their father moved the family to a different part of Kensington. Number 11, Warwick Gardens, is a small house south of Kensington High Street, where the senior Chestertons lived the rest of their lives. Their home was warm and welcoming, the focus of a family life centered upon the Chestertons' beloved boys. Middle class children were usually relegated to the top floor with nurses and governesses until sent away to school, but Cecil and Gilbert Chesterton had their parents' time and affection lavished upon them and were rarely punished. Their friends were welcomed, and their own opinions taken seriously, in spite of the fact that their endless, good-natured arguments broke up family vacations and their mother's parties.

Each boy had his own small den to mess in, drawing, modeling, or manufacturing wooden swords. There was a bookcase filled with his own notebooks in Chesterton's bedroom, while the books he was reading and scribbling in might be found scattered all about the house and long garden.

Young Gilbert was usually thought to take after his father, though his brother said his wit came from his mother, and it was surely his mother he was thinking of when he made his famous statement that it could never be a narrow vocation to teach your own children about the sun and the moon and the stars. It was also her example that led him to see the sexes as two distinct creations, made to complement, not imitate, one another: women the realists, and men the romantic and selfish idealists.

It was this "solemn and star-appointed priestess of democracy and tradition," who fed his imagination with myths about Roman gods, legends about Saint Francis, and fairy tales. To Chesterton, fairyland was nothing but the sunny country of common sense, where he first came to understand the nature of the bright and shining and perilous universe he lived in. His statement in *Orthodoxy* that fairy tales are "spiritual explorations . . . and the most life-like, since they reveal human life as seen, or felt, or divined from the inside," was quoted by Dr. Bruno Bettleheim who worked with disturbed children. He agrees these stories have curative powers, because they accurately reflect reality.

Still, the most important person in Gilbert's childhood was his father, known as Mr. Ed. Living in Kensington, a center for Victorian culture, he was passionately interested in art and well read in English literature. He was also intrigued by science and its practical applications. Having received a good grammar school education, Edward Chesterton had gone into the family business because it was "safer," but he had wanted to be a professional artist. When his sons were still small, he used the excuse of a weak heart to retire from business and spend his days happily at home, becoming his sons' teacher and admiring companion.

In his *Autobiography* Chesterton

remarked that his father's hobbies, many of them artistic in nature, such as watercolor painting, modeling, photography, as well as making tiles, stained glass windows, doing medieval illumination and creating slides for the magic lantern, represented something better than sports which only exercised the body. Chesterton added that on the whole he was glad his father had not become an artist, because it might have stood in the way of his becoming an amateur and spoiled his private career since "he could never have made a vulgar success of all the thousand things he did so successfully." Chesterton's lifelong pleasure in using art to entertain the young was very like his father's.

Mr. Ed also enthusiastically encouraged his sons to make their own creations. He provided the many half-filled notebooks in which small Gilbert tried out titles, or lines from poems and stories, all illustrated with sketches and doodled figures. He sewed his sons' youthful stories into "books," and religiously saved and dated their earliest efforts at writing and drawing, just as he later kept all their press clippings.

Gilbert was slow to talk and even slower to read, although he liked to scribble stories and poems. His earliest writing effort, at age three, called "The History of Kids," written by Aunt Rose at Gilbert's dictation, is a surprisingly action-filled drama about the birth of a prince and his romantic adventures which involve a dragon, a fairy who turns into a boy, Roman soldiers, and Ancient Britons.

But it was at drawing that Gilbert was really precocious. His earliest sketches, like one done at five of men in battle, show movement and detail. A figure of Christ crucified drawn at seven has real arms and legs, with a legend wound round His body which says "gord is my sord and my sheel bikler." Clearly pleased by these signs of artistic talent, Mr. Ed encouraged his elder son to be the family artist, and the praise and importance he attached to his son's earliest efforts must have encouraged Chesterton to assume he was destined to play a role in the world of art.

Mr. Ed was also completely at home in English literature. He made his sons equally fluent and encouraged their prodigious memories. He habitually read aloud to them from the Victorian children's books with their lavish illustrations. They also saw and heard, however, adult books and magazines and the daily newspapers, all illustrated with drawings, not photographs, at this period. Mr. Ed read them Macaulay, Sir Walter Scott, the Brownings, Swinburne, Tennyson, Milton, Shakespeare, and Gilbert's favorite, Charles Dickens.

Their father, the former land agent, also raised them to see that Kensington itself was laid out like a chart to illustrate Macaulay's history. They went on vacations to the seashore at places like Brighton, where the Regent's oriental Pavilion came to symbolize the unexpected in the everyday and where Chesterton learned to love loud winds and hiking. The boys were also taken to hear Gilbert and Sullivan's lively critiques of English society, to see the elaborately staged Christmas pantomimes

with their wonderful mixture of folk and fairy tale, and they themselves "kept" Christmas with great gusto in the traditional Dickensian way with much feasting and song and parlor games.

Indeed, his son described Mr. Ed's even-tempered personality as like a modern, bearded Mr. Pickwick, with good sense tempered with dreaminess, with a tranquil loyalty to other people, and by temperament something of a craftsman and something of a philosopher. His mother Mary Louise, on the other hand, was a queen bee: tart of tongue and quick of wit, prejudiced, impetuous, and ruler of the domestic world of the family which Chesterton called "the home of Jones."

Both parents subscribed wholeheartedly to the Liberal philosophy, born of the French and American Revolutions, "in which the citizen is set up against the state, so that his influence on the state depends upon his independence from it." Their 19th Century Liberalism preached that "the democratic faith is this: that the most terribly important things must be left to ordinary men—the mating of the sexes, the rearing of the young, the laws of the state."

The Monster Schoolboy: 1880 — 1895

Given the family's closeness and the views of Mr. Ed and Mary Louise, it is not surprising that the Chestertons did not send their boys away to school at six or seven to be prepped for one of the English Public Schools like Eton or Rugby. It is also not surprising that Gilbert disliked going to school, even when it was only a short walk down Hammersmith Road to Colet's Court, a preparatory school across the road from the redbricked St. Paul's School for which he was destined.

Chesterton felt a great chasm yawned between his life at school and his life at home, and there are real pictures to substantiate his impression. The first is his portrait, painted at five, of a glowing child with golden locks wearing a bright blue sailor suit. Then there is a black and white studio photograph taken a year later. Gilbert, his head shorn, wearing regulation schoolboy clothes, peers nearsightedly at the camera as he anxiously hugs baby brother Cecil, wearing a long fancy dress with a lace collar. These two pictures show a magical transformation from golden prince to gray pauper, and both were doubtless exhibited at home. So perhaps it is not surprising, either, that as an adult Chesterton happily returned to the more picturesque garb affected by the artist, with flowing locks, cape, and swashbuckling swordstick, to play Falstaff on Fleet Street.

By sending Gilbert and Cecil to Colet Court and then to St. Paul's School, the Chestertons were following the classic English path of upward mobility by educating their sons with those of professional and aristocratic backgrounds. The English Public Schools were expensive private secondary schools, where the classical curriculum flourished, team sports were the major road to peer acceptance, and students were groomed for admission to Oxford or Cambridge and Establishment careers. There were a few very bright, poor boys, like Leonard Woolf, whose barrister father had died young, leaving him dependent upon winning scholarships. Following the unwritten code, Chesterton studied not to appear a brain in class—but he also never really "caught" the English class consciousness, and all his life he remained opposed to the snobbery of elites and old-boy networks.

Chesterton later jokingly wrote his wife Frances that his parents sent him off to school in January, 1880, "when he had drawn pictures on all the blinds and tablecloths and towels and walls and windowpanes," because he obviously "needed a larger sphere." But compared to home, school bored him. He called it that "dull period when he was being instructed by somebody he did not know, about something he did not want to know." He began a pattern of being a poor and inattentive student, who forgot his homework, rarely knew his lessons, and drew or doodled on his books to the point where his teachers were convinced he could not read them. He was big and ungainly for his age, growing more and more nearsighted, messy and unathletic, the perfect dunce and class butt, but his good humor and size kept him from being picked on.

School itself must have been difficult at first, because he did not learn to read until he was nine. When he did, he quickly became a voracious and eclectic reader for the rest of his life, devouring all kinds of literature from pennydreadful detective stories to Sherlock Holmes, Sir Walter Scott and Jane Austen, reading dictionaries, encyclopedias, the daily newspapers, and the Bible.

While he was turning into "that monster, the schoolboy," his family began to take him and Cecil to hear the Reverend Stopforth Brooke preach in Bedford Chapel, Bloomsbury. A former Royal chaplain in the Church of England, in 1880 Brooke quit to become a Unitarian and a Socialist. He taught the Chesterton boys all about what was later called the "New Theology."

The same period saw a very important political development in England. In 1880 the Liberal Gladstone again was elected Prime Minister, and some of Chesterton's earliest cartoons are heads of Gladstone, who, like Dickens, was a Chestertonian family hero. To Edward Chesterton, Gladstone represented the Liberal ideal of a leader with a strong moral sense who wanted men to be their own masters. Gladstone was against the vested interests of the Establishment with their hereditary monopolies in land, government, and religion, but he was not a state planner like the Fabian Socialists, wishing to do good to ordinary people by running their lives for them. As a devout High Churchman, Gladstone also resembled the concerned members of the Church of England like Bishop Charles Gore, who shortly were to found the Christian Social Union to which Chesterton himself and many of his friends later belonged.

Gladstone had come back to power over the issue of an English takeover of the Boer Transvaal in Africa. In 1881, Gladstone redeemed his campaign pledge and gave the Transvaal its freedom. Then, in 1887, Gladstone tried to give Ireland "home rule" and lost office forever, because the big Liberal Whig landowners and Liberal Imperialists like Joseph Chamberlain of Birmingham saw Ireland as "a piece of England." What young Gilbert Chesterton saw was a good man who bravely destroyed both his own career and his party for a principle.

By 1883 Chesterton had gone across the road to St. Paul's School, where he was placed in the second form with boys two years younger. By now he was a "tall, thin, good-looking lad" with wavy chestnut hair, absent-minded and friendly, who liked to hike across London. At St. Paul's he met a group who became his lifelong friends and fans and, through them, his wife Frances.

The first friend he made was Edmund Clerihew Bentley, who was to become a Fleet Street editorial writer and the author of the classic detective story, *Trent's Last Case*. He was in Chesterton's form at school, and one day on the school playground they

began to fight. They were punching one another enthusiastically, until one quoted a line from Macaulay and the other capped it. Instantly they stopped fighting and became friends. They shared a love of literature and a sense of humor that led them into an ongoing artistic collaboration which lasted the rest of their lives.

Bentley and Chesterton now became inseparable. They spent long afternoons at each other's houses where, as Bentley wrote in the dedication of *Trent's Last Case* (to Chesterton, who had dedicated *The Man Who Was Thursday* to him):

> We were purely happy in the boundless consumption of paper, pencils, tea . . . when we embraced the most severe literature and ourselves produced such light reading as was necessary. . . .

Chesterton admired Bentley for his wit and his agility—he shinnied up a lamppost to light his cigarette—and Bentley loved Chesterton for his humor, admired him for his intellect, and looked up to him for his moral leadership, which he exerted by force of character without being aware he had it.

Some of their boyhood projects included a series of adventures about a legendary group of knights, Sir Hugo, Sir Edmund, and Sir Clerihew, with title pages fantastically illuminated by Chesterton. Another was an illustrated romance about their masters at St. Paul's, in which two of the masters were in charge of a third, who was a robot they wound up. Bentley also introduced Chesterton to other boys in

their form, but the fact that Chesterton was very intelligent and a recognized leader among some of his brightest peers still escaped his masters, who wrote despairingly that he belonged in a studio.

In 1890 when Chesterton was sixteen, but in the sixth form with the fourteen-year-olds, he and Bentley became friends with a new student, Lucian Oldershaw, who was destined not only to introduce Chesterton to his wife, but also to become his brother-in-law by marrying his sister. Oldershaw was the son of an actor, with more sophisticated ideas than his friends; he was also a dynamic promoter. Oldershaw decided that since they were not allowed to belong to the top form's literary club, they would form their own; by 1891 the Junior Debating Club, or J.D.C., had come into being. The members met at one another's houses to eat large teas and present papers; Chesterton gave one on Shakespeare's openings. Chesterton became Chairman, while Oldershaw retained the post of Secretary. The original membership included nine other boys, about half of whom were Jewish, and Cecil, who always tagged along.

Next Oldershaw persuaded Chesterton to send a poem called "The Song of Labour" to a Fleet Street weekly paper called *The Speaker*. The poem was accepted and appeared in December 1891. It has the note of high seriousness appropriate to a sincere Gladstonian Liberal, but none of the paradoxical fun and humor usually associated with Chesterton's mature writing. Oldershaw's next project was the

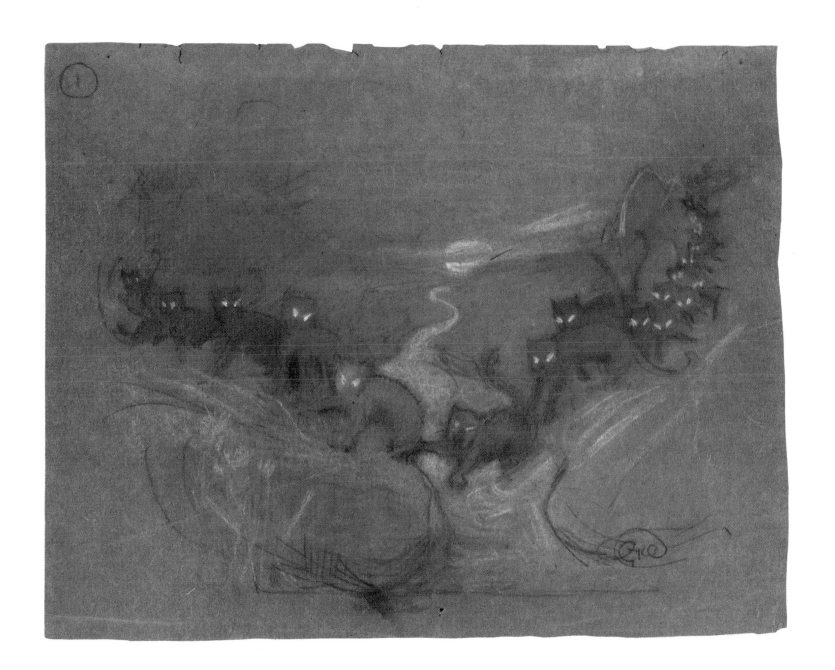

publication of their own printed magazine. In *The Debater*, Chesterton's lighter touch appeared. In an early essay read to the club he announced that "the dragon is certainly the most cosmopolitan of impossibilities." He wrote on the French Revolution like a good Liberal, but also then wrote a "Half Hour in Hades," with illustrations, in which he described the "Common or Garden Serpent," a specimen that a "Mr. J. Milton has discussed at some length."

The J.D.C. had several long-lasting effects on Chesterton's career. In it he made friends whom he kept all his life, through whom he got a chance to write for Fleet Street newspapers. His friends in the J.D.C. were also the first people outside his home to admire him as a *writer* and to help him win public recognition for his work.

Oldershaw now managed to bring *The Debater* to the attention of the High Master of St. Paul's, Frederick Walker. Walker's booming voice, huge red face, and commanding presence seem to have inspired Chesterton's Godlike character Sunday in *The Man Who Was Thursday*. He terrified all Paulites, and Chesterton had been happy to stay beneath his notice, but Walker read their magazine and then stopped Chesterton on Kensington High Street to bellow that he had literary abilities "if he could manage to solidify them." Not content with this degree of fame for his friend, Oldershaw next encouraged Chesterton to write a poem on the set subject, St. Francis Xavier, for the school's annual Milton Prize. Chesterton

won the prize—the first boy ever to do so who was not in the top form.

While the J.D.C. was giving Gilbert a taste for a career in literature, it was amusing itself with another, equally Chestertonian project that required inventive art and a satiric, wacky wit. Doing his Caesar prep, Bentley daydreamed about the chemist Sir Humphrey Davy and wrote a nonsensical quatrain about him, naming the new form a "clerihew" after his own middle name. He and his friends began to produce them; even Mr. Ed wrote a few. Bentley then copied their verses out in a small notebook, which he called the "Dictionary of Biography," because "Geography is about maps/while Biography deals with chaps." Chesterton, the club artist, decorated each small page of verses with lively little line drawings that filled the margins like an illuminated manuscript of nonsense rhymes. He used symbols for the contributors: a dodo for Bentley, a gavel for himself, a pipe for his father, a double pi for Waldo D'Avigdor and a circled 666 for Maurice Solomon.

About 1893, Bentley gave Solomon the little book, then forgot he had done so. Solomon quietly kept it until his death, when his widow gave it to St. Paul's School. Much later, in 1905, Bentley, now a Fleet Street journalist, decided that clerihews might sell, especially if they were illustrated by that popular journalist and writer, G. K. Chesterton. Bentley rewrote from memory as many clerihews as he could remember, added some more, and published *Biography for Beginners* with "40 Diagrams by G. K. Chesterton." This book is probably still the best-known book with Chestertonian illustrations.

In spite of Chesterton's writing successes, his parents still clung to the idea that "art was safer," by which they probably meant professional artists were still in great demand. Photography was not yet a regular replacement for drawn illustrations in magazines, journals, or newspapers. Part of their concern, too, may have come from the grubby reputation of the newspaper world, compared to the comfortably bourgeois lifestyle of the Kensington artists they knew. In any case, the fall of 1892 saw Gilbert, at age 18, leave St. Paul's to begin art school.

After a brief time at a school near St. John's Wood, Chesterton entered the Slade School of Art near the British Museum in Bloomsbury. The Slade School of Art was as prestigious as the Royal Academy, but was considered more modern. Its teaching in the arts imitated the experimental scientific approach which favored using any technique (or theory) that worked. The Slade was part of the University of London, which had been started to educate the Nonconformist, prosperous, urban middle classes, and it had opened in 1871, allowing women to attend classes and the use of live models instead of plaster casts.

Chesterton noted that only a few students really worked at learning art, and, like the others, he preferred to sit about and discuss the theory of art, life, and politics, or attend other lectures. So it was that in an English literature lecture he met Ernest Hodder Williams, whose family owned a publishing house. Much impressed by Chesterton, Hodder Williams later in 1899 gave him his first real chance to write by reviewing art books.

Gilbert's three years at the Slade were very mixed up and unhappy. He suffered through what today might be called an identity crisis, brought on by his late adolescent maturation and by his unresolved doubts about art as a vocation. A hatred of failing his father undoubtedly complicated his confusion, and his interest in a career in art was further diminished by his discovery that he had no sympathy with the Impressionist "ideology" of the period's chief artists like Whistler. While dealing with his own inner anxieties, Chesterton continued to behave as he had always done at school; he scribbled on his drawings and drew all over his lecture notes.

He shared his existential anxieties about doubt and despair with Bentley and Oldershaw, and later in *The Man Who Was Thursday*, he reminded Bentley of the "doubts that drove us through the nights." He also remembered the glory of an afternoon spent with Oldershaw discovering Walt Whitman's *Leaves of Grass*. Whitman's work gave him a literary basis for believing all men had something Godlike about them, and made "green" and "grass" his permanent symbols for everyday reality, which he visually opposed to the Decadents' "green carnation." That artificial

flower, for him, stood for the amoral, meaningless, "art for art's sake" view of the world which the young Chesterton felt pervaded the whole *fin de siècle* society.

Gilbert seems even to have considered suicide, that typical reaction of bright, sensitive adolescents who feel godlike one moment and unsure of anything the next. In many of his poems and stories, Chesterton was to talk sympathetically about the arrogant young who "nearly go mad," and his cure is to teach them that they are not in charge of the universe. His self-doubts are found scattered through the notebooks of his Slade years, which can be dated by his development of an art school "gothic" handwriting that he began to use instead of his sloppy, schoolboy script. A typical notebook has snippets of *pensees* about religion, love, his friends, and public affairs, lists of titles, and some complete poems. Everywhere there are sketches of heads with enormous noses, cartoons of Gladstone, stern rabbits with floppy ears, studies of arms wielding swords, a few cheesecake figures of young females, or sketches illustrating an adventure story. One notebook ends with a huge signature, upside down.

In debating about life with his fellow students, however, Chesterton gradually found that he was playing "Devil's advocate," by refusing to believe that life was meaningless against all the dictates of ordinary common sense. In artistic terms, he decided that if you only saw and painted a white line, because that was all you could see of the actual cow, you were being ridiculous—because the real cow was there. His change of heart crystallized for him one dark afternoon when a fellow student accused him of becoming "orthodox" (or moral) and, to his surprise, Chesterton saw he was right. In a pattern of "conversion through debate" that was typical of his entire life, it would be the arguments of his opponents, the cultured despisers whom he called *heretics*, who would convince him their position was untenable, not the supporters of his own point of view. In this Chesterton was far more of a modern than a reactionary, for he was addressing the views of his own period, not simply falling back on those of an earlier time.

In his last year at the Slade, the other J.D.C. members left London for the universities, making Chesterton once again dependent upon Cecil and the boys his age. With his uncanny ability to pick up ideas, though, Chesterton learned a lot from Bentley and Oldershaw's three years at Oxford. He not only learned about the "elite" activities and attitudes of the University's "gilded youth," but about the prevailing intellectual fashion in Hegelian (Prussian) philosophy and admiration for Bismarckian Germany, both of which he instinctively distrusted.

At Oxford, Oldershaw and Bentley met a former student named Hilaire Belloc, earning a precarious living as a tutor, and word of him must have come back to Chesterton in London. Belloc stood for much the same Liberal position as Chesterton, but he was also half-French (a French citizen until Bentley signed his papers in 1903). Raised a Roman Catholic, Belloc also had the somewhat prickly touchiness of a group still considered subtly "unEnglish." He called himself a Republican. Brilliant, opinionated, and very good company, Belloc made a big impression on these younger men, who, however, decided that they were "new" Liberals, possibly even Socialists, by which they meant they were in favor of some social welfare legislation.

The Defendent: 1896—1902

By spring 1895, Chesterton had finished at the Slade, where his professors suggested he try any career but art. He himself had decided after all to be a writer, but he had not made up his mind exactly what kind of writer. In a sense he never did, even though he called himself a "jolly journalist"—in token, Bentley said, of a moral, not artistic, decision that the most important writing was done in the daily newspapers read by the general public. Like his father before him, Chesterton remained an amateur, or jack of all trades, who was to produce half a dozen minor masterpieces but no monumental *chef d'oeuvre*. His wide audience was itself no less the result of his joking comment that he disobeyed the rule to write for a market and blithely sent the wrong material to everyone. Bentley also humorously commented that Chesterton's definition of a journalist meant writing what he pleased.

More important for the moment, Chesterton had also not figured out how to make a living at writing. He had another poem published in *The Clarion* in April, but he always dated his writing career from that May, just before his 21st birthday, when the editor of the *Academy*, an art magazine, asked him to write a review of a Ruskin Reader. It is interesting that it should have been Ruskin, whose work he knew well and disagreed with in many ways, for

Chesterton was to write a kind of art criticism that had a lot in common with that of Ruskin.

That summer Chesterton also began his first job working for a small publisher near the British Museum. He may have chosen publishing because it, too, seemed "safer" than freelance journalism and would give him time to write. But he quickly found that publishing was demanding, tedious work which paid very badly, and neither gave him much of an entre into the world of writers nor left him time to write. For lack of an alternative that paid, though, he soon changed to a larger publisher, Fisher-Unwin in the heart of Dickens' London, where he worked for six years until 1901, doing editing and promotion work by day and writing poetry and novels by night. Since his parents never kicked their sons out of the nest, he might never have gone into freelance journalism if he had not met his future wife and wanted to earn enough money to get married.

By 1896 his J.D.C. friends like Bentley and Oldershaw had come home from college and began taking Chesterton with them to the many clubs that flourished to amuse young adults. Oldershaw took Chesterton to a meeting of the IDK (or I Don't Know) Club in Bedford Park, a garden suburb known as an artists' colony described by Chesterton as "Saffron Park," a "queer artificial village . . . like a ragged red cloud of sunset." The meeting was at the home of the Bloggs, a family of Huguenot descent who were now devout Anglo-Catholics. There was a widowed

mother, three sisters, all of whom held secretarial jobs, and a brother Knollys. The sisters were not ardent suffragettes, although they were interested in literature and ideas; they worked out of necessity.

On his second visit Chesterton met Frances, the eldest, who looked like a small, poised, Pre-Raphaelite madonna, but calmly and cooly disagreed with everything he said. Frances laughed at Chesterton "with a mixture of admiration and disapproval," but proved to be his link with everyday reality. Above all she had character, rooted in her sincere Christian beliefs, which she practiced in spite of their complete unfashionableness in arty Bedford Park.

When Chesterton met Frances he felt the same jolt of recognition Dante felt when he saw Beatrice: she changed the world. He was born to be a romantic, worshipful lover of womanhood; he was also accustomed to the idea that women were the brighter and more realistic sex. Frances admirably filled both roles for him and served as the unacknowledged model for his heroines, who first make his ramshackle heroes "the Emperors of Creation" by accepting their suit, then become the ruling household deity who has to deal with the romantic young.

Chesterton proposed on their lunch hour on the bridge in St. James Park, but neither family was pleased. Women of their class typically did not work once married, but Chesterton was not making enough to support a wife. Moreover, Chesterton's mother disliked the atmosphere of Bedford

Park. And, while Frances was older than Gilbert and rather frail, Mrs. Blogg clearly felt her daughter could do better, too.

The person most upset was Cecil Chesterton, now seeking work as a cub reporter on Fleet Street, having blithely quit the family business. Cecil was always jealous of Frances' strong influence on his brother. At present he was a Fabian Socialist, so he made fun of her Christianity by suggesting that it was reactionary and romantic, not a realistic approach to the social evils of the day. But it was to be through both Cecil and Frances that Chesterton "met" orthodox Christianity. It was also through these two primary influences that he made close friends in the Christian Social Union, particularly Charles Masterman, another young Liberal journalist, and Conrad Noel, an eccentric Anglo-Catholic priest whose rational arguments for Christianity converted Cecil.

One of the many stories told about their romance is that when Gilbert called upon the Bloggs in the role of an accepted suitor, Mrs. Blogg politely asked his opinion of her new wallpaper. Chesterton got up to take a closer look, then absent-mindedly took a piece of chalk from his pocket and drew a picture of Frances on the wall.

Frances thought Chesterton was meant to be a novelist and to please her he began one which appeared much later as *Manalive*. She was also behind his efforts to find freelance work, which would allow him to quit publishing to write fulltime. Unlike his father, however, Frances never seems to have considered "art" Chesterton's métier.

Then in 1899 her favorite sister, Gertrude, was killed by a bus. Frances became desperately depressed and Chesterton, upon whom she depended emotionally as much as he did upon her, told his parents he must find a way to be married.

That same fall, just as the Boer War began, the J.D.C. threw themselves a stag banquet. Then and there they decided that they must help Chesterton find free-lance writing assignments. Both Bentley and Oldershaw, in addition to reading for the Bar, were doing work for *The Speaker*, a Liberal journal whose editor they knew; this connection eventually bore fruit for Chesterton in 1901. But Chesterton's first real assignments came from his Slade School friend Hodder Williams. These were reviews of books on Velázquez and Poussin for *The Bookman*, again marking him as an art critic, a role Chesterton actually filled intermittently the rest of his life.

In his *Autobiography*, after agreeing that his "centre of gravity . . . had shifted from . . . Art to Literature," Chesterton explained his switch by saying that "having entirely failed to learn how to draw and paint. I tossed off easily enough some criticisms of the weaker points of Rubens . . . I had discovered the easiest of all professions . . ." Within six months he was regularly doing reviews for *The Bookman* on both literary and artistic figures, but he still could not afford to quit his publishing job—or get married.

Appealed to for help, Mr. Ed took matters into his own hands. He talked to Fisher-Unwin about raising Chesterton's salary, but they wanted more of

Chesterton's time. So instead, in order to make Gilbert better known to the editors who could give him free-lance assignments, Mr. Ed decided he must have a book published. Perhaps at Mr. Ed's insistence, or in hopes of regular work as a cartoonist or illustrator, Chesterton chose to use for his first book some illustrated stories in verse which he had made up to amuse Rhonda Bastable, a young cousin of Frances.

Greybeards at Play was not actually published until October 1900, and it did not sell. Chesterton never included it in his list of books, nor did he republish the verses in his *Complete Poems*, but fashion and fancies change. In 1974, at the centenary of Chesterton's birth, the poet W. H. Auden praised *Greybeards at Play*, maintaining that it contained some of the best pure nonsense verse in English "and the author's illustrations are equally good."

When the book still had no publisher by mid-1900, however, Mr. Ed decided they must try to have another book published. This was a collection of poems called *The Wild Knight*, which eventually came out only a month after *Greybeards At Play*. Bentley said he often wondered what the publishing world made of the author of two such different works. He added that a part of the reading public never did understand that Chesterton was in passionate earnest about his ideas but also had an enormous original sense of humor. Moreover, as his career continued, instead of writing some serious and some silly works, Chesterton developed his knack of using humor to make his serious points, and it became the basis of his paradoxical style to turn a truism upside down.

The Wild Knight gained far more critical attention than *Greybeards at Play*. It contains some of Chesterton's best known poems, such as "The Donkey" and "The Babe Unborn," while the title poem is a romantic drama, full of stylistic echoes of Chesterton's favorite poets like Swinburne, Whitman, and Browning. Contemporary poets like Auden dismiss *it* as unreadable, but it was an ancestor of several of Chesterton's later works. It has a close thematic resemblance to *The Man Who Was Thursday*, which also affirmed Chesterton's vision of creation before he called himself

a Christian, and it has a villain who calls evil "good," like Chesterton's fellow students at the Slade. The hero is a Don Quixote-like, whimsical knight, urged on by an energetic heroine.

At any rate, by the end of 1900 Chesterton had finally got his foot in the door at *The Speaker* by doing short pieces on art and literature, which he signed for the first time in the Fleet Street fashion with his initials, "GKC." The best of these essays were published in 1901 in a book called *The Defendent*, where he defended slang, babies, nonsense, rash vows like marriage, and detective stories. He claimed that he was defending the world against those worldlings who despise it and do not see that it must be loved first and improved afterwards.

The Defendent also included Chesterton's famous essay in "Defense of Patriotism," in which he said that "to say my country right or wrong is like saying my mother drunk or sober." He wondered where England, whose poets would walk with Dante, had wandered that she "only bragged about founding colonies and kicking niggers." This article was admired by a bright young provincial editor named A.G. Gardiner who was soon to appear on Fleet Street.

At some time during 1901, Oldershaw or Bentley finally introduced Chesterton to Hilaire Belloc, who had moved to London. Like Chesterton and his friends, Belloc was a pro-Boer Liberal who felt ashamed of their great empire attacking a small nation out of greed. They met one

noon at a Soho restaurant, where they spent the afternoon drinking burgundy and listening to Belloc talk brilliantly and opinionatedly about his favorite topics. Chesterton, in contrast to Belloc, was always the good listener who made everyone feel he was taking part.

Although at this time Chesterton and Belloc shared Liberal, pro-Boer views, the ideas that they became inseparable or that Chesterton was nothing more than Belloc's disciple is an oversimplification which has more the nature of a convenient myth than reality. The very term "the Chesterbelloc" was invented several years later by G. B. Shaw in a debate where he explained why they were *not* alike. The name stuck, first because Cecil Chesterton used it in an anonymous study of his brother published in 1908, and because over many years Chesterton goodnaturedly illustrated over a dozen novels for Belloc. In fact, although they agreed about many things, such as a dislike of the prevailing historical tendancy to attribute English civilization to Teutonic (Prussian) origins, they were ultimately linked in the popular imagination because of their Roman Catholicism.

But Chesterton was always very much his own man. Belloc felt Chesterton had the wrong temperament to be a Roman Catholic convert, and he read few of Chesterton's books because he did not like his style. In an interesting comment made at the time of Chesterton's centenary in 1974, Richard Ingrams said that while Chesterton's contemporaries dismissed him as a child compared with the sophisticated Belloc, time has shown that Belloc with his feuds and dogmatism was the immature schoolboy and Chesterton the one with the instinctive wisdom that let him see the nature of reality.

Chesterton and his friends were breaking into Fleet Street at the moment when it was about to have its "Golden Age." Each paper had a clearcut political and social viewpoint, and even literature was seen as a reflection of the spirit of morality required by art. Queen Victoria had died in 1901 and, as the Boer War dragged on and gave the Liberal party its first rallying cry for a generation, Chesterton began to write reviews regularly for the Liberal *Daily News*.

Since he was now making about 120 pounds a year freelancing, Chesterton quit publishing; on June 28, 1901, he and Frances got married. They lived for a short time in a small house near his parents with a long garden wall which Chesterton thoughtfully decorated for its owner with a crayon mural of knights and fair ladies. Then they moved to Battersea, where Chesterton asked to have brown paper for their wallpaper so he could draw on it.

Chesterton now became a familiar figure on Fleet Street, because Frances, despairing of his untidyness and increasing bulk, costumed him in a flowing cape and soft hat he could not destroy by sitting on it, making him the delight of well-known cartoonists like Max Beerbohm, a "Falstaff in brigand's costume." Chesterton might be seen at a

Fleet Street wine bar, writing his copy and chuckling to himself, or standing stock still in Fleet Street itself, lost in thought. Evenings at Battersea there were beer and sausages for his journalist buddies, Cecil among them, who was now a practicing Anglo-Catholic as well as a Fabian Socialist and becoming friendly with G. B. Shaw.

The Chestertons also saw the Bellocs, living across the river in Chelsea, where Chesterton became a popular figure with their children, playing puppets with them. Through the Bellocs, the Chestertons also met Maurice Baring, son of a wealthy and eccentric family, who was converting to Roman Catholicism.

Mr. Ed had gotten Gilbert a literary agent to handle the business details at which his son was totally inept. Thanks to his mother's insistence on keeping her sons free from materialism, they were both fools about money. Shaw once told Frances she should divorce Chesterton or lock him up as a lunatic because of a contract he had signed.

Then, as the Boer War finally ended, George Cadbury, a Liberal and a birthright Quaker, whose family had become millionaires making chocolate from their Angola cocoa plantations, decided it was his moral obligation to assume total ownership of the *Daily News* in order to give the Liberal Party a Fleet Street voice. His first step as sole proprietor was to hire young A. G. Gardiner as editor.

To Gardiner, journalism was social service and his role a sacred mission to promote the Liberal causes, which were the legislative destruction of landed privilege and monopolies in government and industry, and the disestablishment of the church. He shared the Cadbury family's noncomformist views on temperance reform and was a staunch "Little Englander" who disapproved of imperialism or protectionism. He also wanted to pay members of Parliament, in order to free them to vote their consciences, and he wanted better public education for all.

Chesterton agreed wholeheartedly with this Liberal platform, and Gardiner himself became not only a mentor but a close friend. It was Gardiner who made Chesterton the talk of London when he gave him his "Saturday pulpit," a weekly column in which Chesterton could discuss anything and, as Gardner said, "tap any subject . . . and find a theme on which to hang all the mystery of time and eternity . . . " But Chesterton had really arrived as a literary lion when, in 1902, John Morley, a Liberal Party leader and editor, asked him to write the biography of Robert Browning for the series called "English Men of Letters."

23

The Wild Knight of Fleet Street: 1903—1909

Chesterton's first biography, *Robert Browning*, came out in 1903. It caused much comment of the kind that followed him the rest of his life. He always felt that the way to convey the effect of an author was to sit down and write about him from memory, because "that is what literature is for . . . to be a part of man." He had a prodigious but not perfect memory, with the result that he misquoted Browning thirteen times on one manuscript page, characteristically covered with doodles. The senior editor predicted disaster, but the book was a great success and is still considered one of Chesterton's best studies.

In his book Chesterton followed the structure he used in all his books about artists. Refusing to be too academic, he wrote primarily for his favorite "ordinary reader." He insisted that a man can never be understood apart from the age in which he lived, even when he stood against it, so he first described the period and his subject's relationships to it. Next he gave a few facts, with almost no dates, then drew an impressionistic view of the artist's work. He talked about his subject's craftsmanship, showing considerable technical understanding of his work; finally, he summed him up justly, but with panache. Chesterton invariably caught sight of a truth that was out of fashion. Here he said that Browning was not an obscure, intellectual writer, but one who had found that the ugly and grotesque tell a tale better than static beauty. As a result of this book Chesterton was asked if he would consider a professorship in English literature at Birmingham University, but he politely declined, preferring to remain a "jolly journalist who painted the town red."

In 1903 Chesterton also became involved for the first time in a public debate. He took on Robert Blatchford, editor of *The Clarion*, an old Socialist war horse, defending free will against determinism. Chesterton used his favorite method of attack: reducing his opponent's argument to absurdity. He also used Christian Socialist arguments, with the result that he was asked if he believed in Christianity. He replied "certainly," adding that he also believed that there is a place called Japan and that man is the image of God and therefore all men are equal. Rather than say that he was a Christian, however, his position was that life is logical and workable with these beliefs.

The following year Chesterton wrote his second biographical study for the Popular Library of Art. This was a study of a still living Victorian painter called G. F. Watts, a well-known public figure who had done the murals for the new Houses of Parliament. There is a similarity of structure and tone between Chesterton's *Browning* and *Watts*, both of whom Chesterton had admired since boyhood. These books demonstrated Chesterton's conviction that

an artist was an artist whether he worked in words or pictures, as well as the fact that he took ideas seriously and assumed that, like himself, other artists were expressing a moral purpose in their art. At the same time, none of Chesterton's biographical sketches is like the typical solid, two-volume "life and times" admired by the Victorians: they are far closer in style and intent to Bloomsbury iconoclast Lytton Strachey's impressionistic work, *Eminent Victorians*.

The charge leveled at Chesterton by his brother Cecil in 1908, and repeated often since, that he could only write about people with whom he identified, is shown up in these first two studies. He did identify with Browning, with whom he shared a Liberal, London, middle-class background; but though he admired Watts, he disagreed with much of his philosophy and said so. Watts, however, upon hearing the book read aloud, exclaimed "he has got the key to my intentions."

Both books illustrate what Garry Wills calls Chesterton's "signature of style," in which Chesterton shows familiar things "from unsuspected angles and under new lights of imagination" to let his readers see them with "the innocence of surprise." What these two studies lack, however, is Chesterton's equally famous, pictorial style of "drawing" vivid word pictures to illustrate his ideas.

The years from 1902 through 1909 were a period of high hopes and expectations on the part of all the young Liberal journalists, Chesterton among them.

The Daily News steadily gained readership as the Liberal Party itself became the future, winning a great election victory in 1906 on a platform that now sounds surprisingly "Distributist." To support land reform, Gardiner even resurrected the old Liberal slogan "Three Acres and a Cow," which later was associated with Distributism and Chesterton's cartoon of himself with a cow. The one real disagreement between Chesterton and Gardiner was the latter's great admiration for Germany.

His publisher, George Cadbury, also stood four-square for the Nonconformist Liberal virtues, especially the rights of the individual. But in the public mind the Cadbury family's cocoa plantations exploited the workers like slaves. On Fleet Street their newspapers were called the Cocoa Press, and Chesterton himself long ago had drawn a schoolboy clérihew to illustrate a verse about Cadburys "who never use a bad berry."

George Cadbury, whom Chesterton described as having "an attractive simplicity," found Chesterton's spontaneous wit highly amusing. Cadbury laughed when Chesterton asked if the new revolving door was a cowcatcher, and again when Chesterton started an office rumor that the door had stopped Cadbury from firing one journalist because, no matter how hard Cadbury flung him at the door, it always swung him back again.

The Cadburys used to hold large parties for Liberal supporters, to which his newspaper's journalists were invited. Chesterton described these occasions as

entertaining because they combined the varied elements who made up the Liberal Party, ranging from Whig aristocrats to Nonconformist manufacturers to a few real working-class allies.

The Cadbury-Chesterton relationship was not all business, for it was while visiting George Cadbury at Bournemouth during the Christmas holidays that Chesterton drew the set of six chalk drawings published in this book. Their seasonal history may also account for the fact that they reminded one art critic of English Christmas pantomines. The drawings recently came to Sotheby's in London from the Quaker Peace Service, whose property they had become. What is still unknown is whether they were drawn to illustrate an engaging saga told to young Cadburys and their friends, or to amuse the adults—or both. They presumably date from between 1902 and 1912, for in 1912 Chesterton and the Cadburys had their public quarrel and Chesterton was fired.

In 1905 Chesterton published his first novel, *The Napoleon of Notting Hill*. It is built upon the theme that local patriotism is the only true patriotism, which is lost through empire-building. The story is a whimsical boys' adventure, built upon the Kensington geography of his childhood where the chimney pots rise above the neat townhouse squares, their militant iron railings lining the sidewalks like so many rows of fighting men. The book is also, however, a serious dramatization of Chesterton's conviction that "bigger is not better." In later life, interviewed by his friend and fellow journalist, W. R. Titterton, on what had been his greatest temptation to sin, Chesterton said it was to be Progressive, a world-shaker who only did things "bigger and bigger" until they swallowed up the very thing he loved, "like a certain street in Notting Hill with shops supplying all the spiritual and bodily needs of man."

The Napoleon of Notting Hill catches today's reader by surprise for two reasons: it opens in 1984 and it is genuinely prophetic in ways George Orwell never envisioned. Chesterton was concerned not only about the Orwellian issues of dictatorship, "mind control," and the freedoms of speech and press, but he also

described the London of 1984 as a gray, drab, uniform world, where nothing exciting ever happens, and even the king is elected from the ruling bureaucracy. Then a newly elected king, physically a cartoon of Max Beerbohm (who also enjoyed caricaturing Chesterton), turns out to be a joker. He amuses himself by making the London neighborhoods regain color in everyday city life by building medieval walls, adopting liveries, and raising standing armies.

A humorless fanatic called Adam Wayne adopts the new regime and, as ruler of the neighborhood of Notting Hill, fights to keep a highway from being cut through its territory, threatening to flood London with the Campden Hill waterworks, under whose ramparts Chesterton had been born. Wayne wins, and goes on to conquer all London and rule like a Napoleon until the other neighborhoods combine to defeat him. Wayne and the joker king meet on the last battlefield—and leave as comrades in arms, because the world needs both of them. This conclusion is a typically Chestertonian ending, sane and balanced, after an equally typical Chestertonian wild romance.

The summer of 1904, when the Chestertons were on holiday in Yorkshire, they met another person who, through his ongoing correspondence with Frances, became a considerable influence in their lives. He also gave rise to the series of detective short stories for which Chesterton is perhaps best known today. This was Father John O'Connor, a Roman Catholic parish priest with whom Gilbert hiked

across the moors, talking about the depths of human depravity Father O'Connor had met in his parochial experience. Chesterton was therefore moved to secret mirth in later years when some undergraduates told him the priest was obviously too naive to understand the world. But the actual personality of Father Brown, as he appeared in Chesterton's stories, was not physically like Father O'Connor. Rather, Chesterton described him as "a modern Mr. Pickwick, disguised with a vacant look and the 'ordinariness' of a priest," which makes him another type of Chestertonian "invisible man." In personality and intuition, though, Father Brown shared traits with both Father O'Connor and his creator G. K. Chesterton.

Actually, G. K.'s first published detective story did not feature Father Brown at all. It appeared in *The Idler* in 1904, entitled "The Tremendous Adventures of Major Brown," and then came out in a book of his short stories called *The Club of Queer Trades*, the only one of Chesterton's novels to contain illustrations by the author. The themes of its stories all echo Chesterton's "defense" of detective stories, in which he declared that the romance of modern city life is captured in such tales and that the detective is the true knight-errant. As in *The Napoleon of Notting Hill*, a "sane" sense of balance is again provided by a pair of brothers who are the detectives. One sits home and solves the mystery; the other rushes about London seeking visible clues.

During Lent in 1905, Chesterton "preached" two lay sermons at St. Paul's

Church, Covent Garden. The talks were sponsored by the Christian Social Union. One was called "Vox Populi, Vox Dei," and the other, "The Citizen, The Gentleman, and the Savage." Both reflected Chesterton's emerging Christian beliefs, soon to be immortalized in a pair of his minor masterpieces, *Heretics* and *Orthodoxy*. That same year he wrote the hymn "O God of Earth and Altar." Now, when Belloc had decided to move his growing family to Sussex, Chesterton finally got acquainted with the dominant literary figure of the period, George Bernard Shaw. The result of their growing friendship was that, during their lifetimes, their debates linked them in the public eye far more than Chesterton and Belloc.

In June 1905 *Heretics* was published. It was a collection of G. K.'s *Daily News* columns, dedicated "to my father," whose views on science and progress Chesterton was genially attacking. *Heretics* forms a companion piece with *Orthodoxy*, published three years later, which was dedicated to his mother as the chief prophetess of order and tradition.

Raised a debater, Chesterton always chose argument as a way of getting at the truth. Pictorially, a closed circle was his mental image of the perfect "heretic," whose ideas were quite solid, quite coherent, and quite wrong. He opposed the circle with the cross, whose two slashing lines intersect to produce truth by holding two unreconcilable ideas together. He just as strongly disagreed with the Hegelian dialectic, which moves to higher and higher

syntheses by the resolution of opposites. In speaking or writing, Chesterton's technique was to take his opponent's argument and either stand it on its head or push it to an absurd conclusion. At the same time, he instinctively chose balance, forever taking the opposite side in order to play Devil's advocate whenever he felt an extreme position was winning.

In *Heretics*, for example, his fundamental paradox is his statement that Shaw's new Golden Rule is that "there is no Golden Rule." Then Chesterton made the famous statement which is his basic artistic credo: that "for a landlady considering a lodger, it is important to know his income, but still more important to know his philosophy." He next discussed a number of the famous "heretics" of the day, pointing out that the "unmorality" of art for art's sake had taken root, so that "artists are free to make a hero of Satan and put Heaven under the floor of hell." In the same way, although all colors mixed together ought to make white, in modern paintboxes they commonly produce mud.

As a result, Chesterton cheerfully suggests, men ought to be profoundly suspicious of anybody who claims to be an artist and talks about it a great deal, for art is like walking or saying one's prayers, and the moment it begins to be talked about you can be certain it has come into difficulty. "The artistic temperament is a disease that afflicts amateurs . . . who have not enough power to utter and get rid of the art in their being. . . ." Very great artists are ordinary men like Shakespeare or

Browning . . . and they are didactic; "when we want any art tolerably brisk and bold we go to the doctrinaires who have something to say." Chesterton concludes the book by declaring that he is going on a long journey to look for his own opinions and to find the dogmas he actually believes in, like the fact that leaves are green in summer.

By the end of 1905 Chesterton began to write a second weekly column for *The Illustrated London News*, which he wrote for the rest of his life. Several of his journalist friends, like Belloc and Charles Masterman, had been elected to Parliament in the Liberal landslide, and they gave G.K.C. a ringside seat to watch what happens to a party when it takes power. The Liberals' problem was that they had a mandate for conflicting agendas: for social legislation, for arming against a growing Germany, for educational and temperance reform, and for Irish Home Rule. In addition, several rising young politicians like David Lloyd George and Winston Churchill, both made much of by Gardiner and *The Daily News*, were to prove to be "cuckoos in the nest," who cared more for their own careers than party creeds.

The first recorded meeting between G.B.S. and G.K.C. took place in April in the sculptor Rodin's Paris studio, when Oldershaw and Chesterton came visiting. Shaw seems to have been too busy acting the part of a pundit for Rodin to pay attention to Chesterton, but they began to exchange skirmishes in print and to meet, perhaps with Cecil, who had known Shaw for some time.

Shaw and Chesterton discovered they shared a great love and admiration for the Victorian writer Charles Dickens, who was out of favor with the literary community, and between them they literally put Dickens back on the map. In 1906 Chesterton published his *Charles Dickens* in which, liberally quoting and misquoting, he declared that Dickens was the major literary figure of the 19th century. In a characteristic use of artistic analogies to make his literary point, he added that "although exaggeration is the definition of art . . . moderns permit any writer to emphasize doubts . . . but no man to emphasize dogmas." He also insisted that Dickens' works are simply "lengths cut from the flowing and mixed substance called Dickens . . . a living mythologist whose characters are not always men but gods," a critical opinion that contrasted sharply with Shaw's idea that Dickens wrote about grotesques because the human race looked that way to a superman like Dickens.

Chesterton's second novel, *The Ball and the Cross*, was published serially this year in the Christian Social Union's magazine *Commonwealth*, but it was not put out in book form until 1910. Like *The Napoleon of Notting Hill* and *The Man Who Was Thursday*, its themes of sanity and madness in the modern world are linked with the theme of wonder and romance, which can change the way the world itself is perceived. This novel also has two antagonists who become brothers in arms, a redheaded socialist and a dark Jacobite Catholic Highlander. They try to fight a duel for their beliefs across

England, but are thwarted by different kinds of modern heretics. By arguing, they find that they share an undying love for the freedom of the individual, then are locked up in an asylum for dissidents run by Professor Lucifer who travels in a silver space ship. Another prisoner is an old monk named Michael who leads them all to safety through a fire started by an imprisoned French revolutionary. Lucifer, however, flies away to fight another day, for Chestertonian battles never stay won, but must be fought again in every generation.

In 1907 the Socialist Fabian Society agreed to support a London weekly called *The New Age*. Both Shaw and Cecil Chesterton worked on the project, edited by a journalist named Orage. What is known as the "Great Debate" (between Shaw and Chesterton) started here with an article by Belloc, then one by Chesterton, then H. G. Wells, until finally Shaw got into the act with his famous lampoon on "the Chesterbelloc" in 1908. The series went on to make up more mythical beasts like the "Chestershaw" and the "Shawbox," and during this period European critics often assumed "the Chestershaw" was real, considering Chesterton Shaw's disciple.

At any rate, Shaw did begin to treat Chesterton both as a protege and sparring partner. He tried to get him to write plays, and fussed about his stupidity in money matters. Cartoonists enjoyed drawing the pair of them facing off at each other: both tall, the one skinny, angular, and redbearded, a temperance vegetarian by conviction; the other a pub-frequenter and bon vivant with flying hair and portly girth.

In 1908 Chesterton published *The Man Who Was Thursday*, which is the single novel for which he is best known today. He dedicated it to Bentley in memory of their troubled adolescence, and the novel is a fantastic version of that period, together with an "impressionistic sketch" of Chesterton's own romance.

The novel shows that Chesterton was not just a silly optimist, painting the world bright colors, but someone who had been through the doubts and despairs of the modern world and found a solid basis for belief in Christianity. He drew a symbolic picture of the hell of doubts and the heaven of certainty with his descriptions of the weird sunset with which the story opens and the glorious morning with which it closes—when "Dawn was breaking in colours at once as clear and timid as if Nature made a first attempt at yellow and a first attempt at rose." C. S. Lewis later suggested there was a Kafkaesque quality to this book's nightmare vision, and Kafka himself read Chesterton and commented that his gaiety "was a duty in a godless time."

The Man Who Was Thursday is another Chestertonian adventure story about a quest for meaning. It has a wild chase through London, and a circle of grim anarchist conspirators who turn out to be policemen (or angels), presided over by the towering character Sunday, the Lord of Creation who resembles the High Master of St. Paul's School. The story is also a dramatization of his slovenly autobiography, *Orthodoxy*, which was being written at the same time.

Just before *Orthodoxy* came out, Cecil published anonymously his study of his elder brother called *G.K. Chesterton, A Criticism*. In it Cecil takes his brother to task for playing the buffoon when the world needs serious reformers, and he insists that all Chesterton's ideas came either from Hilaire Belloc or from Frances. But since Cecil had now dropped Socialism and, influenced by Belloc's wife, was considering becoming a Roman Catholic, much of his book is also an attempt to make his brother appear to be on *his* side.

Orthodoxy was written not to refute Cecil, but to answer the critics who said he had criticized others' philosophies without explaining his own. In it, he did not explain or argue whether the Christian Faith is intrinsically believable, but rather how he personally had come to believe it, describing his conversion to orthodox Christianity "in a series of mental pictures rather than a series of deductions." He uses many artistic analogies, and he swings back and forth between examples of visual art and of literature, demonstrating again that they are both what he means by the word "art."

Orthodoxy is another of his "minor" classics which has converted numberless famous and ordinary people to Christianity. Its word pictures rise up in readers' minds to help them remember the arguments. One of the most famous is the opening scene, in which Chesterton describes himself as a yachtsman who discovers

England under the impression it is a new island in the South Seas and lands, armed to the teeth, to plant the flag by Brighton Pavilion. Then he explains that he did not feel a fool at finding out that the Christian faith explained how he "could be astonished at the world and yet at home in it" for "what could be more delightful than to have ... all the terrors of going abroad combined with all the ... security of coming home again?" Later he returns again to the ship image, stating that it made sense to say he was in the wrong place, born upsidedown, or the survivor of a wreck, "one of the crew of a golden ship that had gone down before the beginning of the world."

His discovery of the truth of Christianity had begun in childhood, in the nursery with fairy tales and in the Liberal creed of his parents. As a teenager he learned to separate God from the cosmos and see that the world was His creation. This meant that suicide was not a private right, but a crime against a whole universe —himself. He saw that democracy itself came from the idea of Original Sin, as well as the idea we are created in the image of God—which means that we are artists like Him who throw off our creations to make them free.

He described his Christian under-standing of the cosmos as a creation not vast and void, but small and cozy, "the way a work of art is small in the sight of the artist, small and dear." Christ Himself is drawn as a mirthful giant, whose limbs have been lopped off by the moderns who misunderstand His huge and heroic sanity, "though His coat was woven without seam."

His acceptance of Christianity had developed through debate, for it was the arguments of its cultured despisers, who attacked it on all sides for contradictory reasons, that convinced him of its truth. He said that Christianity took their contradictions, like the colors red and white, and kept them together, side by side, not choosing one over another, nor mixing them to make mud. And in one of his most famous word pictures he described the Church, or "Orthodoxy," as a heavenly Roman chariot behind madly rushing warhorses, who maintained her equilibrium by swerving from left to right, never respectable, but flying thundering through the ages, with the dull heresies sprawling and prostrate, and the wild truth, her driver, reeling but erect. Finally, he suggests that the garden of his childhood was a terrible and wonderful place because it was filled with fixed meanings for him to find out, a place where prophecy after prophecy came true. That is the quality that Christianity recognizes in all creation, which produces wonder and adventure instead of despair by giving you what is literally a second childhood.

The Fantastic Suburb: 1910—1912

In 1909 Frances's brother Knollys, who had converted to Roman Catholicism and become a regular correspondent (like Frances herself) of Father O'Connor, committed suicide. Frances was prostrated by this second untimely death in her family, and Chesterton, whom most people saw as ridiculously dependent upon her, found himself once again very necessary to her. He therefore agreed to move out of London so that they could have a house, he could work at home, and she could finally have a garden. They moved to the town of Beaconsfield, an hour or so out of London. Most of his fellow writers like Shaw, Belloc, and Wells, who did not have jobs on daily papers, had also left London, seeking time

and quiet in which to write, but the move still dismayed Chesterton's many friends on Fleet Street, who loved his company, and it upset his brother most of all.

Cecil insisted loudly and publicly that it was a bourgeois move, engineered by Frances, who hoped to turn Chesterton into a tame man of letters and possibly win him a title. Cecil ignored the fact that his brother was working very hard and getting tired and overweight, as well as the fact that, living in Beaconsfield, Chesterton never did quit being part of the working press. He continued to write two columns a week, which took the efforts of his entire household to get to Town on time.

Fleet Street itself was no longer the

happy place it had been. Like the members of the Liberal Party, their press was being "disciplined" to keep the Liberals in power. Papers like *The Speaker* had closed down, and the profitable London papers were all Conservative. Even *The Daily News* was in trouble, and George Cadbury had begun to talk of selling it if his son Henry could not make it pay. Under this kind of stress, Gardiner, Chesterton's chief editor, felt under constant crossfire, as his Liberal journalists grew angry at being asked to toe the party line or obey the orders of the Cadburys.

As early as 1907 Chesterton had gone on record protesting the fact that he had not been allowed to defend a Liberal MP who had denounced the open sale of titles to fill the Liberal Party war chest. This practice, long known in politics, was being brought to new heights by "the party of reform." Chesterton then begged to be allowed to write a letter to the editor in support of the M.P.'s protest, and had done so, but the seeds of trouble were sown. It did not help his state of mind to have other journalists routinely call the Cadburys "slaveowners," or to have Shaw taunt him with being "Cadbury's property." About the time he moved to Beaconsfield, Chesterton wrote a sad and bitter poem called "When I Came Back to Fleet Street," in which he called his fellow journalists "the prisoners of the Fleet," to remind his readers that there had been an ancient prison on that site.

Chesterton's next biographical study was on a living subject, his friend the well-known playwright and Fabian Socialist,

George Bernard Shaw. This book proved to be one of his most brilliant, giving a picture of the differences between the two debating opponents—the one "orthodox," the other "heretical" in Chestertonian terms—both linked by a real concern for society, a gift for humor, and dramatic ability on and off the stage. Like all his biographies, this book also drew a sharp picture of Shaw in relation to his times.

Chesterton described Shaw as a Puritan, a Progressive, and an Irishman, who was really a respectable gentleman of the middle classes who disliked the poor and wanted to replace them with useful supermen. He explained that Shaw insisted on carrying his principles to absurdity instead of using moderation and common sense, and, beneath Shaw's public mantle of "metaphysical jester" (a title Chesterton, too, is often given), Chesterton detected a very moral mystic crusading for his Life Force. Chesterton gleefully completed his portrait by saying that while most people either agreed with Shaw or did not understand him, he understood him but totally disagreed with him. He described Shaw as a sternly ascetic saint, saying that he was "like the Venus de Milo, all there is of him is admirable."

Shaw slyly tried to discredit the book by saying he was "proud to have been the painter's model," but then pointing out its factual errors and ridiculing Chesterton's insights. Yet the study is an orderly and straightforward account both of Shaw's work and his development as a displaced Irish Protestant, which makes very understandable how, in the 20's, Shaw should quarrel so bitterly with Chesterton for becoming a Roman Catholic and why Shaw should also be impressed by the efficiency of regimes like Soviet Russia or even Nazi Germany.

Tremendous Trifles, one of the best known of Chesterton's many collections of newspaper columns, came out about the same time. In it G.K.C. used his storylike style, with each episode (or essay) built upon a paradox integral to the main idea, not a mere verbal twist. Some of these essays sound bitter, reflecting his dismay at the sight of his Liberal Party struggling to survive at any cost, but they also destroy the thesis that Chesterton's political and social ideas were fixed in place by 1900 and never changed. They make understandable his comment later that he had not left the Liberal Party but it had left him.

When the Chestertons moved to Beaconsfield, they first rented a house called "Overroads." There was a pasture across the road where they liked to picnic under a large tree. Later they bought the field and built a studio, which they made into their home, Top Meadow. Top Meadow is a rambling, redbrick and stuccoed cottage with a large garden where Frances grew flowers for Chesterton to spear in search of ideas.

G.K. enjoyed being part of a town. He wrote about the old and new towns of Beaconsfield, where there were two barbers and two inns, the White Stag and The Saracen's Head, all of which he patronized.

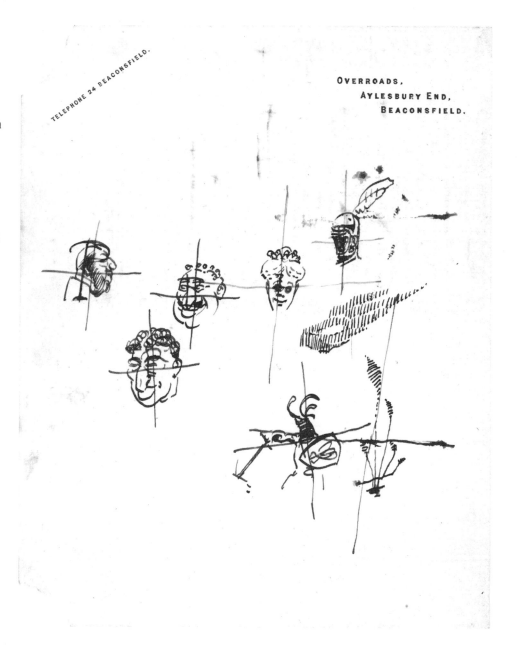

TELEPHONE 24 BEACONSFIELD.

OVERROADS,
AYLESBURY END,
BEACONSFIELD.

39

The Chestertons acquired dogs and cats as pets, and hired a series of neighbors for secretaries, none very efficient until Dorothy Collins arrived in 1926. They often visited other people and had many guests, for whom Chesterton drew cartoons and gave productions in his toy theatre. One such epic was a political satire, a dramatization of the Socialists' Minority Report on the Poor Law, with puppets of Fabians Beatrice and Sidney Webb. He drew place cards for parties and sent silly notes like "GKC's Famous After-Xmas Cards" or the "I Am Late for Everything" series.

The Chestertons' favorite visitors were the children of family and friends. These nieces and nephews all remembered climbing upon Chesterton's knee to demand he draw pictures and make up a story to match. Mornings when he reluctantly went off to write, strange things might happen, like a colorful paper bird sailing out the window, or a giant sea serpent sliding down the front stairs. When his nephew Peter Oldershaw was sick he received a continued story about a boy who pulled a rope and found it attached to a BEAR.

The newly completed poem "Lepanto," which was shouted by men in World War I as they went over the top, was first read to eight-year-old Nicholas Bentley for his approval, while older children had Chesterton's help putting out a family newspaper, "just as soon as he finished some unimportant stuff for the *Daily News*." At one time there was a regular Saturday game built around the Valiant and Judicious Order of the Long Bow. The

Grand Master was the Holy Uncle, Banker to the Order, who provided all members with wooden swords, shields decorated with their special blazons, and eight arrows. In the Charter, the Holy Uncle swore to keep combat from being lethal, to provide an assembly for redressing grievances, and to protect the windows and sensibilities of parents.

Most of Frances' efforts to get Chesterton's work done on a more orderly basis were defeated by his own absent-mindedness until she had Dorothy Collins' help. This was the period when, away on a lecture tour, Chesterton telegraphed her "Am at Market Harborough. Where should I be?" to which Frances sensibly replied "Home." Chesterton really appears to have enjoyed the weekly fuss when guests or secretaries madly bicycled to the station with his columns, or Frances called to have the train met in London.

Having grown up in a home with his father busy about his many projects and his mother in charge, Chesterton liked living that way. In *What's Wrong with the World* he was to describe a happy home as one in which "The queen is in the counting house, counting out the money, The king is in the parlor, eating bread and honey." He had a deep, instinctive hatred for the industrial and clerical employment of women outside their homes—work that he felt misused their talents,—and, like Belloc, he also equated the suffragette movement with the idle upper-class women who were bored by "mooning about" in their large, servant-filled houses. He saw the home itself as the proper arena for the feminine "generalist" who had the whole world as her responsibility, compared to the "narrow male specialist" with a mere job.

Another General Election was called in 1910 to force a showdown with the Conservative House of Lords, which kept vetoing Liberal legislation. Still a convinced Liberal, Chesterton called it the most important election of his lifetime. This "revolution without an R" was hailed at the time as a great Liberal victory, but historians now agree with Chesterton in a different sense, because this fight contributed to the disappearance of the Liberal Party and the rise of the Labor Party in its place.

At the same time, like many of his friends, Chesterton was more suspicious of his own party leadership. Here he was influenced by Cecil and by Belloc, who had won re-election as an independent, disgusted by the "slave" status of a Backbencher who was expected to vote the party line. Besides this lack of freedom to criticize their own chiefs, Belloc and Cecil argued that the leaders of both parties had gone to school together and were so intermarried that it seemed to make a mockery out of so-called "two party" government. In 1911 Belloc and Cecil Chesterton published a book called *The Party System* in which they described this old boys' network. They also began to make personal attacks on Liberals they felt were too interested in their own careers. One of their favorite victims was their old Christian Social Union and Fleet Street

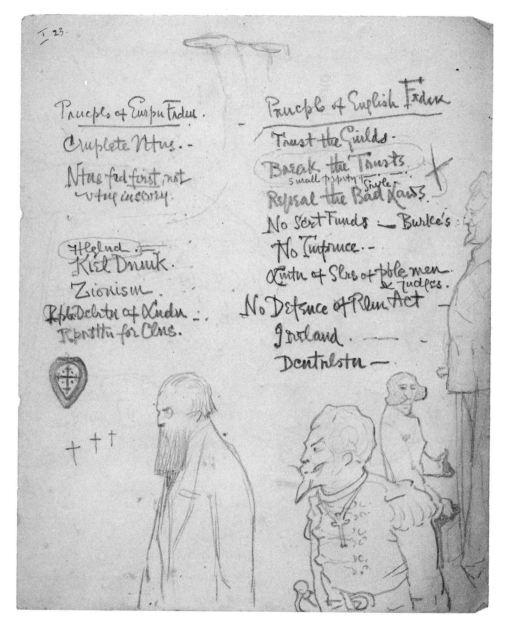

41

friend, Charles Masterman, who had married into a prominent Liberal family and was now a minor Liberal minister.

Edward VII died in May, 1910, just as Halley's Comet made one of its historic passes over England, and Chesterton published *What's Wrong With the World*, his first book of social comment not written originally as newspaper columns. Like many of his nonfiction books, it was an answer to a recent book by Charles Masterman called *The Condition of England*; in other words, it gave Chesterton's side of another "debate." Masterman had tried to describe what England needed to make her well again, but he was quite patronizing about the middle-class suburbanite who did not understand the aristocratic principle of *noblesse oblige* and felt he was being taxed by big government to help the poor. Chesterton, who saw himself as a middle-class suburbanite, and always disapproved of telling the other fellow how to live his own life, responded by suggesting that Masterman should start with the cure, not the disease—or a few ideals instead of merely pragmatic solutions. He suggested that Masterman remember that, to the ordinary Englishman, his "Home of Jones" was really his castle, the only place where he was still free to do as he pleased. He added that "the idea of private property . . . one man, one house . . . remains the real vision and magnet of mankind."

What's Wrong With The World is vintage Chesterton: readable, quotable, casual, and friendly compared to Belloc's study called

The Servile State. Chesterton writes as one of the ruled, not one of the rulers and, as usual, he argues by reducing a concept to absurdity. One of the best is his graphic description of the old Tory and the old Socialist, Hudge and Gudge, both of whom wish to reduce men to slaves. The Conservative convinces himself that "slums and stinks are really very nice and the habit of sleeping fourteen to a room is what made England great," while his lean vegetarian Socialist counterpart waxes eloquent about public housing projects which he calls "hives where mankind can live like the bees, happy in one universal bedroom."

G.K.C. suggested that society, an invention of man, can be put forwards or backwards like a clock, and he pointed out that everyone is a teacher and that all education is dogma; there are no uneducated people, only people educated wrong. He illustrated this concept with a delightful parable about a confused little boy first educated by a Nonconformist, then by a crook like Fagin, next by a vegetarian Socialist, and finally by a pacificist, all of whom in succession would teach him their conflicting doctrines.

He ended the book by ridiculing the Progressive who has a Puritanical (or Calvinist determinist) vision of Utopia, in which man's history is settled before he is born. He blamed this approach on the Pagan (or Prussian) north and, by contrast, he asserted that many of the largest efforts of history, "like the French Revolution or the Roman Catholic Church, have been frustrated in their full design and have come down to us [like] ... half-built villas abandoned by a bankrupt builder." "This world," he insisted, "is more like an unfinished suburb than a deserted cemetery."

Once again, Chesterton was intuitively aware of the "advanced" ideas in the air. That very December, as the first Post-Impressionist Exhibit was mounted in London, Virginia Woolf declared a new age had dawned and human character itself had changed. She complained that the older writers (like G.K.C.) made her feel their work was incomplete unless she joined a society or wrote a check, so she and her group of Bloomsbury artists instead looked back to Henry James as their model for their generation's version of Chesterton's old *bete noir*, "art for art's sake." Chesterton had already noted that Henry James "so admired the past" that his very characters were no more than ghostly figments of his imagination, but Woolf's comments illustrate the social fact that by 1910 evolutionary Liberal reform was dead and that the modern world was already in place: not only in French art, in Russian music and ballet, but also in such scientific advances as airplanes, the telephone, psychoanalysis, and the movies.

Into this pre-war period of rising revolutionary expectations, in which society itself again seemed to be coming undone, Chesterton was asked to do another biographical study for the Popular Library of Art. This book was to be on William Blake, whom he admired as a draftsman

but felt uneasy about as prophet or poet. His book on Blake comes across today as a prophecy aimed at the Bloomsbury group's aesthetic theories, which were to become the postwar credo but which for Chesterton were really a repetition of the hated theories of his school days. The book also makes a fine companion to his earlier one on Watts, for here Chesterton talks about the atmosphere of the eighteenth century; there, he had described the nineteenth century. In both books he used the artists to describe their eras, and seized the opportunity the book gave him to defend "Christendom's" moral vision.

During 1911 Shaw and Chesterton held another round of their "Great Debate" which was very well-publicized. They actually spoke several months apart to the Heretics Club at Cambridge University. As always, the sheer physical contrast between the two was itself newsworthy, for Shaw appeared on time, spick and span in his knitted Jaeger suits, and lectured eloquently in his melodious Irish voice. Chesterton habitually arrived disheveled, late, and in haste, dropping notes on bits of paper. He spoke conversationally in a surprisingly high voice, and his speech was disjointed and full of jokes about himself. But once the formal lecture was over, Chesterton more than held his own, both in quick repartee and in fast responses to questions from the floor.

Shaw told the University students God had died in the 19th century, but they were not to worry for he was inventing a new Superman with his Life Force. In rebuttal,

Chesterton told them that Christianity was still the true religion but that he did not believe "for one minute that England is a Christian country." He added that Shaw was something of a Pagan, and like all Pagans, a very fine man—as far as he went. The London newspapers picked up the debate, and Shaw was so delighted with the publicity he organized more debates in London, all the time nagging Chesterton by letter and in person to write a play.

In June, 1911, Belloc started his own weekly, called *The Eye Witness*, and hired Cecil Chesterton as his assistant editor. G.K.C. himself only contributed some satirical poems and "drinking songs" like the one about Noah who didn't care where the water got "if it doesn't get into the wine." It was an unsettled period with many strange political alliances, and *The Eye Witness* supported contradictory groups in the course of its editorial battles against "Prussianism," the House of Lords, social engineering, welfare programs, rich international financiers, Liberal Party leaders, Jews, and women suffragettes. Some of its unlikely allies were the Syndicalists, Guild Socialists, and those Conservatives eager to arm against Germany. Its writers were friends from Fleet Street like W. T. Titterton, Ada Jones (an emancipated woman reporter given to causes and rows), and the Dominican Father Vincent McNabb, who preached a simple life without machinery and, together with the Bellocs, husband and wife, had a great deal to do with the fact that Cecil Chesterton soon joined the Roman Catholic Church. Nasty verbal abuse of ministers and other public figures was *The Eye Witness'* stock in trade, together with a dramatic but very real concern for ordinary people affected by unfair laws. Belloc now stood against any welfare legislation because it destroyed individual choice.

That July Chesterton published *The Innocence of Father Brown*, the first book of stories about his amateur priest-detective. These stories have proved to be the most durable of all Chesterton's writing, and in Father Brown he created a memorable character who is closely identified with his creator. Written fast, these stories linger in the reader's mind as much for their gorgeous word pictures setting the scene as for the moral atmospheres they match; scenes like Hampstead Heath where, "under a perfect dome of peacock-green sunk into gold amid the blackening trees and the dark violet distances," Father Brown talks philosophy with Flambeau, who plans to steal the blue cross. The Father Brown stories also illustrate many of Chesterton's social and political concerns: his hatred of big business, his distrust of a governing elite, and his dismay at megalomaniac artists who "play God" with others' lives.

The short story form was ideally suited to Chesterton's talent for telescoping events to concentrate on one central idea. His plots often derive from Poe's classics, like *The Purloined Letter*, but as in the story "The Invisible Man," where a "socially invisible" postman is the murderer, G.K.C.'s plots also deal with moral realities, described with Chesterton's own brand of wit and humor.

The character of Father Brown himself was "fitted out with features meant to be effective in that setting . . . a commonplace exterior . . . that contrasted with unsuspected vigilance and intelligence . . . ." While Christianity defines the atmosphere of the stories, the criticism that they are pure Roman Catholic "propaganda" is really an identification of Father Brown's profession with that of his narrator's, as well as public reaction to Chesterton's postwar conversion to Roman Catholicism.

Chesterton's next major work was his long narrative poem, *The Ballad of the White Horse*. It retells the story of King Alfred the Great's fight to keep the pagan Norsemen (or Germans) from taking over Christian (or Roman) England. The poem is really a parable for his own day. Chesterton saw the new King George V as a kind of Alfred, or younger brother, working hard at a job for which he had not been trained.

The poem also expressed Chesterton's lifelong belief, first expressed in his prize poem about Saint Francis Xavier, that it did not matter whether an individual won or lost if he fought as hard as he could, and that no battle is ever won forever but, like the White Horse, must be cleaned again and again. The last few verses point another moral in which Chesterton, the journalist, sarcastically states that the new pagans are the press.

Poems like this one, written in ballad style for public reading, are no longer the fashion and are therefore labelled by critics "Victorian" or "primitive." But in its day this poem carried as sharp and compelling a view of the world as any of Chesterton's admired satiric verse. The poet Auden stated that the varied views of the human condition expressed in it by the pagan leaders "could not be condensed without loss;" he also comments that, like Chesterton's sacramental Christian view of the world, his pagans base their pessimism upon their observation of the natural and visible world. Serious or not, in England this one ballad was so widely known that it was quoted on the front page of *The Times* the day Crete fell in World War II and Britain stood alone against Hitler.

In 1912 Chesterton published a rewritten version of his earliest novel, begun in his publishing days. *Manalive* was another Chestertonian celebration of the joy of being alive and the need for romance and adventure in everyday life. This gospel is preached to a group of modern young people who live in a London rooming house, and the prophet is Innocent Smith who blows around the world on the wind of the Holy Spirit. He lands at Brighton to claim the country, rewoos and remarries his own wife, and attempts to kill an intellectual whom he hears preaching pessimism, who quickly runs away. He is "tried" in the boarding house as a madman but, like a true Chestertonian hero, Smith proves to be the only sane person there. In keeping with G.K.C.'s growing disillusionment over how public affairs are managed, this novel also sounds a new note by suggesting that moral problems should be solved privately at home, a theme which reappears in his postwar fiction.

One of Chesterton's best books of what might be called "art criticisms" was also published in 1912 in another popular series. *The Victorian Age in Literature* provides a marvelous introduction to Victorian literature. It is also the book in which he sums up his own Victorian background, points out its moral and artistic deficiences, but admits that he, too, in many ways is still a Victorian.

He describes the age from Macaulay to Huxley as a compromise between the rising forces of rationalism and the waning faith of an earlier age. This Victorian era represented an alliance of middle-class religion and economics, joined to aristocratic political forms. But it was attacked by his real heroes, the Victorian revolutionaries like Dickens, Ruskin, Carlyle, and Cardinal Newman. Their attack splintered the Victorian world into socialism and imperialism, or into Shaw and Kipling. The book helps to explain why Chesterton developed the religion his father did not have, but it is also full of masterly one-liners about individual artists, like "The Oxford Movement was a bow that broke when it had let loose the flashing arrow that was Newman," or "Hardy was a sort of village atheist brooding over the village idiot."

Belloc now published *The Servile State* in which he expounded the classic "radical" Liberal views with which he and Chesterton had been raised. But Belloc also agreed with the Fabian historian R. H. Tawney that it was the Tudor agricultural enclosures which began the destruction of the freedom of the small land holders, leading to their conversion into the wage-slaves of industrialism. It was this book, based on 19th century Liberalism, combined with the ideas on workers' rights Belloc had learned from Cardinal Manning and Pope Leo XIII's famous Encyclical Letter "Rerum Novarum," that provided most of the ideas for what was later called "Distributism." Belloc now resigned as editor of *The Eye Witness* and Cecil Chesterton happily took over as editor—just as a real Liberal Party scandal broke into the open on Fleet Street.

The Marconi Days: 1912—1919

The Marconi Affair had begun in 1911, when Parliament decided to establish an imperial telegraph system. The Marconi Company made a bid, accepted provisionally by the government, but advertised as settled by one director, Godfrey Isaacs, an English Jew and brother to a Liberal cabinet minister. Isaacs then reorganized the American Marconi Company and brought back to England American shares, whose value depended upon the English contract. His brother, the cabinet minister Rufus Isaacs, bought some on speculation, as did Lloyd George, who was Chancellor of the Exchequer, and the Liberal Party for its "war chest." When the Marconi contract was put before the House of Commons for formal debate by Charles Masterman, Fleet Street suddenly published its suspicions about the ministerial dabbling in the stock. Cecil outdid the other Conservative newspaper in his language and abuse, but the Liberal press, afraid of destroying their own party, were as divided as the Liberals themselves.

At this moment *The Eye Witness* folded and, encouraged by Ada Jones who was working with him, Cecil went to Mr. Ed for money to restart the paper under the name of *The New Witness*. Cecil next began to attack Godfrey Isaacs (the only non-minister) for his business dealings. The Liberal ministers had sued a French paper for suggesting they dabbled in *British*

J. b. (Slun).

Marconi stocks (the line they also took in Parliament) but in February, 1913, Godfrey Isaacs sued Cecil Chesterton for libel.

Ever afterwards, G.K.C. divided modern history into Pre-Marconi and Post-Marconi days, because it was then he learned that the Liberal Party's own leadership would lie to save themselves. Cecil's libel trial itself was something of a farce, because he refused to believe that there was a legal law of libel and treated the court like a debating society, trying to be his own lawyer and score points against two of the most brilliant Conservative lawyers of the day, Sir Edward Carson and F. E. Smith. Cecil lost both his case and his nerve, for he unexpectedly backed down in Court about his accusations and got off with a stiff fine when he might have gone to prison. But he and Ada Jones always acted as if he had won his case instead of making a fool of himself.

On the other hand, Chesterton and his family had been terrified Cecil would go to prison, and it was the dreadful sight of his adored and arrogant brother in the dock that led to Chesterton's final, fatal row with the Cadburys and the *Daily News*. Fearing to bring down the Liberal Government and worried about his own job, Gardiner had refused to print much about the Marconi Affair, even though it was his own Party's ministers who had been lining their pockets at public expense. Chesterton therefore wrote a poem, "The Song of Right and Wrong," which was published in Cecil's paper. It contained the line "Cocoa is a cad and coward"—an unmistakable allusion to the Cocoa Press.

More in sorrow than in anger, Gardiner remonstrated with him over this gross outrage against his associates in journalism and asked him to "correct" the impression the poem made. His letter made it clear Chesterton was being asked to resign. Chesterton wrote back to apologize and to resign, saying that he had not meant anything personal but could not continue to take the money of a man who thought he had insulted him. Chesterton added that the Cadburys had never been anything but nice to him and he had never accused them of being hypocrites. He ended with the significant comment that he believed his friends right about politics, but wrong about people.

Chesterton is usually accused of being obsessed by the Marconi Affair, as well as of showing anti-Semitism because the Isaacs were Jews, but historically the affair was a major turning point for the Liberal Party. The very ministers, like Lloyd George and Rufus Isaacs, who were saved from resigning in disgrace were to be the country's postwar leaders who wrote the Treaty of Versailles, and also destroyed the Liberal Party. In addition, Cecil, as if he had to prove he was no coward, enlisted in World War I and died of a war-related illness in 1918. It is not so surprising, therefore, that when Godfrey Isaacs died in 1925 Chesterton for once wrote a very bitter "Open Letter to Lord Reading" (Rufus Isaacs) telling him he was lucky his brother was dead.

During the remaining year before the war, there was a very successful production of G.K.'s play *Magic*, written in answer to Shaw's demands, and the only play of Chesterton's performed in his lifetime. Continental critics, in reviewing this play, called Chesterton a literary disciple of Shaw; in contrast to Shavian supermen, though, *Magic* told again the Chestertonian fable of the artist who plays God and must be redeemed by becoming an ordinary man. This time he is a wandering magician who gives in to temptation and turns a red lamp blue to teach a brash skeptic a lesson. The most amusing character is a Shavian duke given to malapropisms, who evenhandedly gives money to start a new pub *and* to a league to put down drinking. In this same year, 1913, Chesterton also took part in an elaborate benefit for the Dickens Society, a re-enactment of the trial of John Jasper from Dicken's *Edwin Drood* in which he played the judge in robes and wig, and he spent a silly day making a cowboy movie with G. B. Shaw and Sir James Barrie.

He also published a novel called *The Flying Inn*. It is one of many "invasion" novels written then, including an early one by P. G. Wodehouse. Chesterton's version features a Turkish invasion of England set up by a peer who has become a convert to Islam. Lord Ivywood, who lives with a "harem" of faddish society women in a Moorish castle rather like Leighton House in Kensington, is defeated by an Irish soldier of fortune, a pub owner with a portable keg of wine, a journalist, and a very intelligent dog, Quoodle, named after the Chesterton's pet. During this period also, to make up his lost *Daily News* income, Chesterton began to write for the socialist *Daily Herald* whose voice was as shrill as the times themselves, but he quit when the paper's editor stayed pacifist during the war.

When war finally broke out in August, 1914, England had been on the brink of civil war, brought on, Chesterton thought, by the breakdown of the Gladstonian public morality which had protected private rights. Although Chesterton is often accused of being a boyish lover of blood and thunder and he certainly had always mistrusted the Germans, he was neither sentimental about the war like H. G. Wells, who decided this was going to be the war to end war, nor angrily pacifist like Shaw. Chesterton commented simply that the war was being fought only because the alternative was worse. It would not bring an ideal Beaconsfield nor a New Beaconsfield, but it would keep Beaconsfield Beaconsfield, without being overshadowed by Berlin.

Chesterton was physically unfit to fight, but he was asked to join a group of writers under Charles Masterman producing propaganda aimed at drawing America into the war. He wrote a number of books and pamphlets, like *The Short History of England,* aimed at showing that the English and German civilizations were not the same. His second Father Brown collection also appeared that fall, with a sharp story called "The Purple Wig" in which a cowardly editor changed his copy to suit his proprietor.

In the late fall of 1914, Chesterton suffered a complete breakdown. By Christmas Eve, he had fallen into a coma from which he did not emerge until Easter, 1915. Belloc took over his *Illustrated London News* column, and since no one was allowed to see him, even his parents and brother, Frances spent the time sitting with him, reading the proofs for a new book of his poems.

Father O'Connor wrote her that Chesterton had once said he wanted to convert to Roman Catholicism; then he came to Beaconsfield. Frances, however, refused to let him see Gilbert until he was awake and in his right mind. She was terribly distressed about the episode because she knew that Chesterton's parents had disliked Cecil's conversion at the time of the Marconi Trial and would blame her for allowing G.K.C. to follow suit. She was also personally against the idea, but she always wanted Chesterton to have what he wanted. When Chesterton recovered, though, none of them spoke of it again.

By 1916 Cecil had fought his way into the army and married Ada Jones on the strength of it. He left his little weekly newspaper in Chesterton's charge, hoping his brother could save it with the greater drawing power of his name. Being an editor was a chore Chesterton felt totally unsuited to (and had no time for), but Cecil's call for help was one that he could not but obey. He spent the rest of the war running Cecil's paper and writing more propaganda books for Masterman's office. He even made a trip to Ireland to help promote volunteers (instead of the draft) and his articles written there were later published in *Irish Impressions*.

The war ended in November, 1918, but that December Cecil Chesterton died in a military hospital in France. His death left his brother at once bereft and saddled with the permanent responsibility, which he saw as a sacred trust, of trying to keep Cecil's "voice" alive on a Fleet Street increasingly dominated by great chains. Bentley commented that his old friend would never have retired to become the Sage of Beaconsfield, dwelling in the past, but to run a newspaper from Beaconsfield presented Chesterton with heavy financial and logistical problems.

The Red Cross of Saint George: 1920—1926

The postwar world was not a happy place. The peace treaty was being written by the leaders Chesterton mistrusted. Lloyd George, who had run the wartime coalition government, now held a quick election to keep power, but many Liberals, including Charles Masterman, lost their seats. There was civil war in Ireland and an economic slump in England that meant there were no jobs for the returning veterans.

It is small wonder that when the doctor said Frances must spend the winter in a warmer climate, Chesterton left Cecil's paper temporarily in Ada Chesterton's charge to take a trip set up by Bentley. Bentley now worked at the *London Daily*

Telegraph, which agreed to publish Chesterton's impressions from abroad, later collected in a book called *The New Jerusalem*. The very last article Chesterton was to write, however, seriously discussing the problems there would be if Palestine were given to the Jews for a homeland without being fair to the Arabs, was considered too anti-Semitic and was not run by *The Daily News*.

The Chestertons spent the winter of 1919-1920 traveling through France, Egypt, and finally Palestine itself. G. K. enjoyed the whole trip, but it was Jerusalem that thrilled him the most. It was only a few years since Jerusalem had been freed from the Turks by the dashing English hero T. E. Lawrence of Arabia. Now he found that

it was a little medieval walled city, set upon a hill, looking much the way it must have when the Crusaders were there, once again flying the Red cross of Saint George.

Chesterton's childlike delight in Jerusalem, lightly frosted with snow like a Christmas card, also came from his intense preoccupation with his own future. Cecil's death not only left him with the moral obligation to keep alive the spirit of opposition in Fleet Street, but it made him feel a great need for the support and the discipline of what he was to call the "iron ring of Catholic responsibilities." In other words, at this time he was thinking very seriously about joining the Roman Catholic Church, which now seemed to be the only church prepared to fight for the central core of Christianity. His language suggests that he saw this step, which would upset not only his parents but Frances, as "taking the cross" like a crusader to defend a Christendom cut loose from its traditional moorings in the pessimistic and godless world. His attitude was also greatly affected by the modernist sterility Chesterton perceived as coming from the leaders of the Church of England, which seemed to be leading them back into a solipsistic Protestantism.

Back in England, G. K. finally took back his *Illustrated London News* column from Belloc and published his wartime articles on Ireland in *Irish Impressions*, in which he reacted as sympathetically as always to the Irish demand for independence and their own culture and religion. *The Superstition of Divorce*, another group of his pre-war articles on marriage and divorce, also appeared. Its focus was on the family as the cornerstone of society, not, said Chesterton, because a family is a group in which one may do as he pleases, but because it is a group with which he must get along.

That fall of 1920, partly to replenish the coffers of his hungry little newspaper and partly to distract Frances who hated to have him devote so much time to it, the Chestertons set sail for their first trip to America. Although Frances did not like the United States very much, their tour was highly successful. Chesterton was always affable and made "good copy" with his impromptu remarks—like the comment that he did not plan to go farther west than Chicago, for, having seen Jerusalem and Chicago, "I think I shall have touched the extremes of civilization." He spoke out strongly against Prohibition, which he saw as another instance of the rich telling the poor what to do without obeying the law themselves, and he consequently enjoyed meeting Sinclair Lewis at Marshall Field's and co-plotting a mystery story over a bottle of bootlegged whiskey.

At home again the Chestertons converted their studio at Top Meadow into their home, using the old stage as the dining room. Chesterton published *Eugenics and Other Evils*, yet another group of articles written before the war about what today might be called "social engineering." In 1922 his father died, leaving Gilbert the additional burden of managing the family's affairs. All through this period he had also been corresponding with Maurice Baring

and with Father Ronald Knox, both English Roman Catholic converts. By July 1922, he had finally made up his mind to join their church.

Chesterton was well aware of the fact that many people would misinterpret his decision as a retreat to "reaction and medievalism" and refuse to listen to him any longer, while others who thought his politics and social ideas old-fashioned would act as if he had been a Roman Catholic all along. G. K. himself felt as if his country and his party had both deserted him; he saw this step as not only swearing allegiance to Rome, the very font of Western Civilization, but also, at the same time, as defending a community that was very like a small, beleaguered "nation" to which he could be fiercely loyal. Afterwards he was to write his widowed mother that "I think, as Cecil did, that the fight for the family, and the free citizen and everything decent must now be waged by the one fighting form of Christianity. . . . I have thought this out for myself and not in a hurry of feeling. . . . I believe it is the truth."

He was received into the Roman Catholic Church on Sunday, July 30, 1922, in the temporary chapel in Beaconsfield's Railway Hotel. Only Father John O'Connor and Father Ignatius Rice of Douai were there, together with a weeping Frances. When the news became public, there was a great deal of reaction: Baring rejoiced, Belloc was disapproving and disbelieving until it was done, and Shaw felt bitterly betrayed.

Busy as he was with Cecil's weekly,

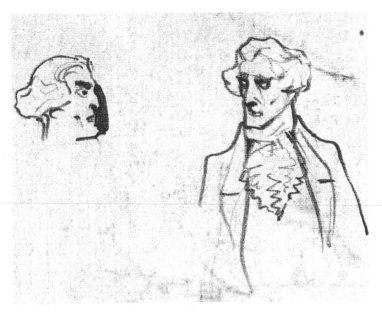

G. K. continued to publish other books as well. *What I Saw in America*, his articles about the previous year's trip, appeared in September. He insisted international friendship could only grow if countries respected one another's differences, for most wars have been between little nations who lived too close for comfort. His wartime poems were published in *The Ballad of Saint Barbara*, including his famous poem celebrating the rebirth of Poland and his bitter "Elegy in a Country Churchyard" contrasting the venal rulers of England to the men who died in the war.

His next novel is one of a group known as the "Distributist" novels. Like many of his later books, *The Man Who Knew Too Much* is made up of short stories with the same

protagonist, who is interested in small property and individual freedom. The hero is a member of the ruling elite who use him as a scapegoat, but afterwards begin to carry through a few genuine "distributist" reforms. Throughout the book a young journalist is being "educated" by observing the scene, and finally echoes the hero's call for revolution "because it might do no harm to blow the whole tangle . . . to hell."

In October, 1923, Chesterton wrote about one of his enduring favorites, a boyhood hero, Saint Francis of Assisi, whom he described as a troubadour of God who acted out the romance of Courtly Love. He approached Saint Francis "through what is picturesque and popular" in order to give his reader the "consistency of a complete character." His short portrait is drawn very simply, with the clean colors and statuesque quality of a Giotto painting, but the book shines with Chesterton's image of the new day which Saint Francis brought: "While it was yet twilight, a figure appeared silently and suddenly on a little hill above the city, dark against the fading darkness. . . . He stood with his hands lifted . . . and about him was a burst of birds singing: and behind him was the break of day."

Through all his efforts, including the use of his share of his father's estate, his Father Brown stories, trips, and other books, Chesterton had managed to keep Cecil's newspaper afloat, but in May 1923 it failed. Since he would not, could not, agree to losing a "free voice on Fleet Street," most of his friends recommended that he broaden the paper and make it more his own. Shaw even suggested calling it "Chesterton's," but added that G. K. would have to write a Father Brown story once a week to support it.

Chesterton's resolve was further strengthened that December when another election was held and, for the first time in English history, the Labor Party formed a government with the help of what was left of the Liberals. At the same time, he was facing a literary generation gap. Disillusionment with the war and the peace had led younger intellectuals to adopt T. S. Eliot's poem *The Waste Land* as their own world view. Chesterton saw their reaction as another round of the decadent pessimism he had fought as a young man, just as the "New Left" was heir to the Fabian Socialist of his youth.

Feeling that he must go on speaking for Western Civilization's enduring values, he ran by invitation in three elections for honorary head of a major university, defiantly calling himself a Liberal. He lost the elections, but his moral message got across to some of the young, among them Dorothy L. Sayers, C. S. Lewis, even T. S. Eliot and W. H. Auden, who "reconverted" to Christianity and then paid tribute to his influence. There was also the group of younger Roman Catholic converts like Evelyn Waugh and Graham Greene who inherited the more sympathetic intellectual climate towards religion (and Roman Catholicism) which Chesterton helped to create.

But the fact he had become a Roman Catholic also made Chesterton both a "medieval reactionary" and "unEnglish" to the "Left," typified by the writer Frank Swinnerton, while Irish writers like Sean O'Casey abused him for not being Roman Catholic (or Irish) enough. G. K. had anticipated this two-edged sword and, in a group of apologetic essays called *The Thing*, he cheerfully explained that he had felt it his duty not to avoid the accusations of his fellow Protestant and agnostic countrymen when his co-religionists were being pelted with insults for saying their religion is right.

He also decided that he must spend his time, money, and energy re-establishing Cecil's little paper; renamed G. K.'s *Weekly* it appeared officially on March 21, 1925. It was his creation, for he wrote a large part of it, edited it, soothed the rows among the staff and board, and wrote many Father Brown stories to support it.

In restarting the newspaper, Chesterton had to tell Cecil's widow that the paper could not support two Chestertons as editors. She decided that he was jealous of Cecil's memory, but she continued to write for it. G. B. Shaw on the contrary was enraged that Chesterton had sold himself into journalistic slavery for a mere 500 pounds a year, and Maurice Baring would not serve on the board, having no money to spare and feeling it a waste of Chesterton's talents, an attitude Frances also shared. Chesterton appealed to his old friend Titterton, now enthusiastically religious and Distributist, to come help him out. Titterton, who adored Chesterton, later described G. K.'s weekly editorial trips to Town, calling them "Little Gilbert's Half-Holidays."

Chesterton would arrive from the train, pockets stuffed with papers, cigarillo in one hand, sword stick in the other, cloak flapping, announcing himself with a chuckle. His copy was always covered with drawings, for, as Titterton said, he liked to draw as much as he liked to talk, but he would settle down in the tiny office and write whatever else was needed to fill up the paper. The weekly board meetings were usually rows and worries over money which Chesterton soothed as he sat doodling. He kept insisting that he was the worst editor in the world, but at one board meeting publicly told Frances that the paper must go on.

In 1922 Chesterton again began to help Belloc with his chronic financial problems by illustrating a novel a year for him, and this continued the rest of his life. He really co-authored these "Chesterbelloc" novels, since Belloc often wrote Chesterton, begging him to do the illustrations because it would help him write the story, and appending a list of "situations." Dorothy Collins has described how Belloc would then appear at Beaconsfield with a few ideas and the two men would spend the day holed up in the study until teatime, laughing and making up the story as Chesterton drew the illustrations. Belloc took the illustrations (anywhere from 25 to 40) home and then wrote the book. Chesterton also drew more clerihew cartoons for Bentley and occasionally drew cartoons for his own G. K.'s *Weekly* as well.

In 1925 he published his second collection of "Distributist" short stores. These are each based on a familiar saying, like "Eat your hat" or "Set the Thames on fire," not unlike the illustrations he drew for Rhoda Bastable's *First English Phrase Book* when she was a child. In *Tales of the Long Bow*, though, an agrarian revolution is finally carried out by a group of middle-class yeomen in Lincoln Green, led by a certain Robert Owen Hood.

His *The Everlasting Man* also appeared in 1925. This was Chesterton's contribution to a public postwar debate between Belloc and H. G. Wells. Wells had published *The Outline of History* in 1919, to illustrate his usual "gospel" of salvation by history in which man progresses from slime to world government. Typically, Wells gave Greece and Rome little space because they were "early" civilizations, and his most vicious attacks were aimed at the Roman Catholic Church, which had publicly condemned him for "free love."

Chesterton decided to answer Wells directly by writing a popular version of the "sacred quest of mankind." He opened by saying that there are two ways to get home: one is to stay there, and the other to go around the world until we come back to the same place. Then he drew a picture of a boy whose farm stood on those vast valleys with sloping sides along which the ancient White Horses of Wessex are scrawled, who went on his travels to find something like a giant. When he was far enough from home, he looked back and saw that his own farm

63

was part of such a gigantic figure, "on which he had always lived, but which was too large and too close to be seen."

The first half of the book describes the man in the cave, who is not like other animals because he is an artist who draws pictures, which makes him the image of his Creator. G. K. ends the first half of history with the great age of paganism in the late Roman Empire, which died "when the good things in society no longer worked." At that particular moment in history God was born in the cave, and "[there] stands up an enormous exception . . . really and right in the middle of historical times, there did walk into the world . . . the Man Who Made the World." With His coming, the world was re-created, so that on Easter Sunday He walked again in the garden, disguised as the gardener.

Critics said that Chesterton's portrait of Christ was that of a Chestertonian hero, full of a Dickensian love of the ordinary people, humorous and sane in a mad world—to which Chesterton replied that was Who he found in His story. Chesterton is also accused of defending the Roman Catholic Church when often he is talking about Western Civilization itself, which he always called "Christendom." He agreed that his aim was to put religion back into history, where it could be seen as a motivating cause and guiding spirit for man's actions, but he would have none of blurring the lines between the world's religions, because the world is not divided into "shades of mysticism or forms of mythology, but between the men who bring the Christian message and the men who have not heard it or cannot believe it."

Postwar economic conditions had brought back plans for a General Strike. Titterton now persuaded Chesterton to finish the novel about a strike he had begun in 1914, and *The Return of Don Quixote* came out serially in G.K.'s *Weekly* in 1925. The novel is often taken to prove Chesterton had retreated to the "Roman Catholic" Middle Ages, but the plot concerns a representative group of modern young men and women, including a neo-Fascist, a Socialist, a Roman Catholic, a Suffragette, as well as some "detached observers" whom Chesterton calls "Don Quixote" and "Sancho Panza," and who appear to be the author's real spokesmen.

When a "medieval League of the Lion," started at an aristocratic houseparty held at a coal mine owner's home which was once an abbey, is subverted by the neo-Fascist, the others fight it. A General Strike is put down, but the chief Chestertonian spokesman, Douglas Murrell, says the result will be an England with a history that is too simple, "too black and white, dividing the classes." The real General Strike in May 1925 was declared illegal and ended quickly, but for many young writers like W. H. Auden and Stephen Spender, it was the watershed that led to their public and moral political involvement in the 30's.

To save the still struggling G.K.'s *Weekly*, Titterton had the idea of making it the official organ of the newly established Distributist League, which had branches in different parts of England. Chesterton became president, but he was really too busy to do much except support the "cause" in his paper, which was helped by League subscriptions but never as much as needed.

His first postwar Father Brown collection appeared in 1926, featuring several stories about dead American millionaires; Father Brown himself began to sound more and more like Chesterton, the narrator of other stories like *Tales of The Long Bow*. The focus, like that of *The Return of Don Quixote*, had also shifted from a public to a personal morality. Father Brown works to save an individual soul, like the artist who plays God in "The Dagger with Wings," instead of trying to reform society's viewpoint as he did in "The Invisible Man."

The Return of Don Quixote: 1926 — 1936

On All Saints Day, 1926, Frances Chesterton joined the Roman Catholic Church. She always hated to have it said that she had done it because of her husband, despite the fact there must have been an element of that in her decision; but she hated still more the publicity her conversion caused

In 1926 Chesterton published some of his lead editorials called "Straws in the Wind" from G.K.'s *Weekly* in a book entitled *The Outline of Sanity.* He wrote that when people ask "What are we coming to?" I answer, "Monopoly. I believe the cure for centralization, either with capital in the hands of a few capitalists . . . or a few politicians . . . both destroy liberty . . .

depends upon widespread ownership of property . . . The critic of the State can only exist where a religious sense of right protects his claim to his own . . . pen or his own printing press."

He said he did not think state action in itself was immoral, but that there was a definite doctrine of the universe and the nature of man behind his newspaper, because "the old morality, the Christian religion, the Catholic Church believed in the rights of man . . . The new philosophy utterly distrusts a man." It was this position that led T. S. Eliot in his obituary to say that Chesterton's social and political ideas might seem to have been totally without effect, but they were fundamentally

GK's WEEKLY

EDITED BY G.K. CHESTERTON

DECEMBER 7 - 1933
VOL. XVIII.   No. 456

Registered as a Newspaper   SIXPENCE.

215

"God forbid that I should Glory
Save in the Cross of Christ."
Prussian Motto

GK's WEEKLY

EDITED BY G.K. CHESTERTON

NOVEMBER 7 - 1935
VOL. XXII.   No. 556

Registered as a Newspaper.   SIXPENCE

"Why should Labour want the Red Shirt or the Black Shirt, when it can attain to the Boiled Shirt at last?"

Christian and he had done more than any man of his time to maintain "the existence of that important minority in the modern world."

Another collection of his poems, *The Queen of Seven Swords*, describing the Virgin Mary as the great White Witch who saves man from the pagan curses of old folk-and-fairytales, was published that December by the new firm of Sheed and Ward, run by Maisie Ward, daughter of the prominent Roman Catholic editor, Wilfred Ward, and her husband, Frank Sheed. It was Maisie Ward who wrote perhaps the best-known biography of Chesterton after his death. G.K.C. had publicly admired the Virgin Mary since adolescence, and an English legend about her was a major element in *The Ballad of the White Horse*, but many critics now assumed this was all typical Roman Catholic "Mariolatry."

In May, 1927, Poland invited the Chestertons to come and see the results of ten years of nationhood. G.K. had always had a special love for Poland, which he saw as an embattled outpost of Christendom defending Europe against the infidels, as well as a small peasant or "distributist" country resurrected from the dead. He, Frances, and Dorothy Collins, who was like a daughter to them, accepted the invitation and they spent five weeks being treated like visiting royalty. Chesterton always remembered an officer's welcome, in which he said that while Chesterton was a great friend of Poland, whom he had defended often in his paper, he would not say that he

was the chief friend of Poland, "for God is our chief friend."

Chesterton's *Collected Poems*, (without *Greybeards at Play*) was published next, and by September, 1927, *The Secret of Father Brown* had come out. It contained the short story "The Chief Mourner of Marne" which is anthologized almost as much as "The Blue Diamond" or "The Invisible Man," and it is the story typically cited to prove that his Father Brown stories are straight religious propaganda. Far more helpful, however, for understanding Chesterton's art, are the prologue and epilogue, in which Father Brown is interviewed by an American reporter. He tells the reporter he detects crime by getting inside of a man "until I am thinking his thoughts." The reporter replies that he doesn't know if Father Brown would make a really good criminal, but he ought to make "a rattling good novelist!" Chesterton also wrote a play about one of his heroes, Dr. Samuel Johnson, but it was not performed in his lifetime.

During this period Chesterton was at work on two other books which are often paired together. Both do represent a summing up of what had made his life complete, but neither book is very trustworthy about facts or dates. One is his biographical study of *Robert Louis Stevenson* published in 1927; the other, his *Autobiography*, finished a few months before his death and published posthumously.

The Stevenson book is Chesterton at his best, showing an artist against the background of his age. The parallels with his own life are close because Stevenson, too, studied art before he became a writer. This fact gave Chesterton one more chance to attack the pessimistic *fin de siècle* atmosphere of the Slade and the immorality of "art-for-art's-sake." Chesterton praised Stevenson for refusing, like himself, to join the writer's movement towards formlessness which is "very much of a novelty but not much of a novel." He slyly suggested that the moderns just leave Stevenson "in the dead past along with Cervantes and Balzac and Dickens," adding that "the best poetry of [Edith] Sitwell is a sort of parody of *A Child's Garden of Verses.*" Stevenson, too, saw the world in bright, romantic colors and used the toy theatre as a way of defining the limits of art. Unlike Stevenson, though, Chesterton did not spend his childhood as a sickly, solitary invalid, nor voyage to the South Seas in search of health or sanity.

The British Broadcasting Company was established in 1926, with a state monopoly of the airwaves which Chesterton as a Liberal had publicly denounced. In 1927, however, Titterton, still seeking financial help for G.K.'s *Weekly*, got G. B. Shaw to agree to debate Chesterton on "Distributism" under the title "Do We Agree?" The debate was to be held in a public hall where they could sell tickets and, as in pre-war days, Belloc was asked to moderate. Then another young staff member, Gregory Macdonald, arranged for the B.B.C. to broadcast the debate to which Shaw generously agreed—asking

only if there really was a Distributist League or if it were just Titterton running in and out with a flag? Both men performed brilliantly, and who "won" depended upon the point of view of the listener, while Belloc as moderator uttered an Orwellian prophecy that civilization was built upon coal but would shortly float upon oil.

By 1929 the Liberal Party had made and lost its last attempt to regain office, the Labour party was again running the government, and the Great Depression was just around the corner. Chesterton published a collection of stories called *The Poet and the Lunatics* with another of his "mad" artists as hero, but Gabriel Gale is waging war against the insane world. Gale ties a young curate who thinks he runs the universe to a tree so that he will learn how helpless he is, and he stands on his head when the heroine accepts his suit, but the book ends with the suggestion that England now is ruled not by lunatics but by crooks.

In 1928 the mystery writer Anthony Berkeley founded the Detection Club, and G.K.C. was asked to be its first Ruler. He had a fine time officiating at club initiations wearing a scarlet and black Mandarin robe and a Fu Manchu pill box hat, surrounded by the other members carrying the "implements of their trade." He also joined them in writing *The Floating Admiral*, a parlor game kind of mystery, where each author wrote the next chapter, trying to use the characters and clues left him by the previous chapter's writer.

One of Chesterton's best known books of Roman Catholic apologetics, *The Thing*, came out in 1929. In it he attacked the arrogance of men like H. G. Wells or Dean Inge of St. Paul's Cathedral, who said that by joining the Church he had stopped thinking. To this accusation Chesterton replied that it was clear to him the modern world was living on its Catholic capital and using up the truths that remain to it out of the old treasury of Christendom. He added that the Protestantism of the Reformation was believed by almost no one and, having come from a Protestant home, he was brought up to cling to the Protestant feud, not the Protestant faith. By contrast, the Church itself simply stood for "sanity and social balance against heretics who were very like . . . lunatics." He added that these moderns are very upset that a religion they left for dead has come to life and, in defense of the idea of the papacy, he suggested that it would be good for the world to have a permanent official in some central city to represent peace and be the basis for agreement among the nations.

The Chestertons and Dorothy Collins spent the fall in Rome. Chesterton not only had a private meeting with Pope Pius XI, at which they talked about his *Saint Francis of Assisi*, but he also met Mussolini. His impressions of the latter were published later in *The Resurrection of Rome*, where he suggested Europe itself was upside down because it had been letting its heels (Germany) run its head (Rome). But he ended by saying sadly that he wished the world had a real white flag of freedom which was neither "the red flag of Communism nor the black flag of Fascism."

When Belloc turned sixty in 1930, his many friends threw an enormous party to celebrate. Chesterton served as master of ceremonies and said the occasion was something like a cross between a day of judgment and a dream, because all the people there were known to him. There were supposed to be no speeches, but someone whispered to Chesterton that it would be nice to thank those responsible and, when he did, that person thanked the man next to him, and so on, until everyone there had spoken.

Four Faultless Felons, another collection of stories told to an American reporter by men who seemed to be crooks but were really heroes, came out in 1930. Their stories are parables about extremism; the religion of science; a family business that is really England; and a media-event in a small country, where the mere report of a revolution causes a reformation.

That October the Chestertons and Dorothy Collins set sail again for America. He was scheduled to give two lecture series at Notre Dame, as well as travel and give talks and keep up his columns. His lectures were jammed; his delivery, as usual, a bit disorganized, but his wealth of information and insights, his genial manners, even his impressive bulk with his shaggy mane of wild hair and his cape slung over his shoulders, contributed to his appeal. It was his spontaneous wit, though, that won his audiences, like the time he said he was not really as big as he seemed but was being amplified by the mike.

Stories are still told about the Chestertons around South Bend, where the students especially loved the fact he came to their football game against Navy (and wrote a poem about it) the year Knute Rockne coached them to an undefeated season. Frances Chesterton figures in some legends as his keeper, worried that he would overdo or overdrink—both of which concerns were probably well-founded. On November 5, G.K.C. was made an honorary doctor of laws in the first special convocation ever held at Notre Dame.

On the lecture circuit, Chesterton also debated religion with the famous Chicago lawyer Clarence Darrow, who had won the Swopes Case and defended Leopold and Loeb. Chesterton found Darrow a poor adversary, with a literal, Bible-Belt idea of religion that made him talk about things like Jonah and the whale. G.K. was far faster at thinking on his feet, for when their mike failed he cheerfully called out, "See, Science is not infallible."

Returning to England, however, Chesterton repeated his position that the two countries were separate and should remain so. He disliked America's materialism and worship of wealth, though he liked the mass production of inexpensive Fords because they stood for America's great virtue—which was that she really was a democracy where the citizens feel equal.

Historian Arnold Toynbee has called

1931 "Annus Terribilis," because the Wall Street crash spread to Europe and it seemed as if "the Western System might break down." Many more of the younger intellectuals, infuriated by the Conservative "do nothing" approach, turned sharply left, but many also became pacifists. Chesterton attacked this position as vehemently in his paper as he did the ineffectual League of Nations, which he called a Tower of Babel built on the old hope of creating supermen. Paradoxically, these younger writers who considered Chesterton "Old King Cole" now saw the arts in terms of political and social policy, just as his generation had demanded a public art that reflected morality. If T.S. Eliot was one of their mentors, it was W. H. Auden who became their spokesman, and by the 40's both Auden and Eliot had joined the Church of England.

On Christmas Day, 1931, Chesterton began another career. He broadcast for the BBC on Dickens and Christmas to the United States. He turned out to be perfect for radio, and by October the BBC had hired him to do a regular program reviewing books which made him widely known to what his sister-in-law waspishly called his "new and idolatrous following." G.K.C. however, was not impressed with his own importance. Both Mrs. Chesterton and Mrs. Blogg had died in 1932, and before Dorothy Collins could stop him Chesterton had burned most of the papers in his father's study. He did agree to spend some of the money he inherited to build the

larger study at Top Meadow for them to work in.

His book on *Chaucer* appeared the following April of 1932. Again his critics took his subject to prove that he was medieval at heart, but his chief point was that in Chaucer's time the intellectuals and the people still spoke the same language. Chaucer, therefore, could be read by everyone, the way Chesterton wanted to be. This was what he meant by a spiritual democracy, that shared a Christian world view with its sanity and common sense. At the same time, when the Nazis took over Austria, he felt back in the world of "Lepanto" with the Turks at Europe's door, and in *All I Survey* he wrote very soberly that a man in the later Roman Empire . . . under Diocletian . . . " would be quite at home |here| . . . and prepare for death as a martyr."

In 1932 he published his articles from the recent trip to America in *Sidelights on New London and Newer York*, and in 1933 he published still another of his "minor masterpieces," *Saint Thomas Aquinas, The Dumb Ox*. Like his *Saint Francis of Assisi*, it was meant to be read by beginners who were not Roman Catholics, let alone Thomist theologians, because "the biography will lead to the philosophy and the philosophy to the theology."

Typically, Chesterton set out to examine Aquinas in his life and times. He clearly felt a sense of identity with Aquinas, the polemicist who was also a poet, who was very big, very bright, and a bit of a "dumb ox" at school. He said that Aquinas reaffirmed the Incarnation by bringing God back to earth, and by using Aristotle to provide the materials he needed to build a philosophic structure to defend all creation against the Manichees, who hated the world. This is almost a description of the work Chesterton had set out to do, and, again like Chesterton, Aquinas felt that "man is not a balloon going up into the sky, nor a mole burrowing . . . in the earth, but rather a thing like a tree, whose roots are fed from the earth, while its branches . . . rise almost to the stars." The Thomist tradition was both the guardian of sanity and the only basis for political reform. When the book had come out, Frank Sheed met Etienne Gilson, the brilliant Thomist theologian, in a Parisian bookstore, and Gilson told him the book was so good it made him despair, for "I have studied Aquinas all my life but could never have written such a book."

In 1934 the Pope made both Chesterton and Belloc Knight Commanders of Saint Gregory, and Chesterton was elected to the prestigious Athenaeum Club. He also published *The Scandal of Father Brown* and *The Well and the Shallows*, a collection of Roman Catholic apologetic essays put out by Sheed and Ward. It is not an account of his conversion but a defense of the Church against the modernists, in which he puts his faith in what he calls history, not eschatology.

By the beginning of 1936 Chesterton was chronically worn out or ill, often with bronchitis, although his doctors thought the real problem was his heart. Dorothy

Collins drove him and Frances on a trip through France that spring, trying to help him relax. They visited both Lourdes and Lisieux, with G.K. tunelessly singing Gilbert and Sullivan songs as they went along. Back home, on his last BBC broadcast on March 18, he poked fun at T. S. Eliot's poem "The Hollow Men" by declaiming: "And they may end with a whimper/but we will end with a bang."

During that spring he began to fall asleep at his desk and finally was put to bed, while Dorothy Collins tried to keep word from leaking out. To Bentley's amazement, the Press did respect his need for quiet. Because of this secrecy, though, Chesterton's death on June 14, 1936, was not only a surprise to the world but a dreadful shock to his many friends.

That same evening, Bentley broadcast a tribute to Chesterton over the BBC saying that his friend was:

> not only one of the most greatly gifted, but one of the most beloved men of his time . . . [who] had in him the stuff of a great artist in the commonly accepted meaning of that word. There was nothing he could not do with a pencil or, by preference, with what, in our boyhood, we called a box of chalks . . . He honored simplicity and kindness [for] as he once put it, kindness . . . is God's last word.

The Artist and the Lunatics

The Art of G. K. Chesterton

This book is called "the art" of G. K. Chesterton to underline a basic Chestertonian paradox. He called himself "a journalist" because he saw ideas or notions "wrestling naked ... not dressed up in a masquerade as men and women." He insisted that he could not help "being a controversialist" who saw art's purpose as propaganda, for, he said, "Art, like morality, consists in drawing the line somewhere." But fifty years after his death, it is apparent that when Chesterton tossed off those "fleeting sketches meant ... to help his fellow men exercise the eye until it learns to see the startling facts that run across the landscape as plain as a painted fence. ..."

he himself was looking at the world like an artist.

Any portrait of Chesterton the artist, however, must talk about his "art" in several ways. First, there is his actual artwork, represented by his many drawings, cartoons, and doodles like those that illustrate this book. They all clearly reflect his lifelong preoccupation with visual art as a medium of expression and a way of releasing his thoughts; they also demonstate his skill at drawing a firm line. Secondly, there is his verbal art which, like his drawings, was typically tossed off in haste to make a point or illuminate an idea.

Finally, underneath both methods of

artistic creation there is his bedrock moral purpose. It was served by his genius for popular communication, for Chesterton the artist's final intention was always to make his vision of the universe visible to his ordinary reader. All three aspects of his art—visual, verbal, and philosophical—are needed to understand and appreciate his artistry.

In both words and pictures, he made his point with a strong, firm line that outlined a central figure (or idea) against an impressionistic, often fantastic, background. His verbal penchant for pushing an argument to absurdity was the literary counterpart of the visual effect he created by cartooning his message. In both mediums, by using artificial limits like the frame of the toy theatre, he gave focus and clarity to his ideas. In this way Chesterton was able to draw the moral so starkly or whimsically that its point cannot be missed by anyone.

In visual art the key to Chesterton's development lies in his childhood. His earliest apprehension of the world around him began with his memory of his father's toy theatre, which predated both the death of his sister and the birth of his brother. The toy theatre formed his artistic imagination, for in all his work Chesterton kept the clear, sharp view of a child, where the relationship between the visual and the moral is intimate and organic. But this view was not one-dimensional, for the toy theatre's definite outline also suggested to him the things not pictured, like "the backs of the houses of which I saw only the fronts. . . ."

He was also greatly moved by colors, like Olive Ashley in *The Return of Don Quixote*, where "all her first thoughts . . . had been coloured . . . from the beginning. Certain pointed shapes, certain shining colours, were things that existed first and set a standard for all this fallen world. . . . She caught her breath at the mere memory of certain wavy bars of silver or escalloped edges of peacock green."

Chesterton seems to have used color itself as a kind of second language, and G. B. Shaw once wrote him that, just as he could not describe himself without knowing music, so Chesterton could not write his own spiritual history in ignorance of painting. This Shavian judgment can be justified by Chesterton's play, *Magic*, where the crucial action onstage is the lamp that turns from red to blue.

Encouraged by his father, the young Chesterton resembled Gabriel Gale in *The Poet and the Lunatics*, who "could not see a large blank wall without having an uncontrollable appetite for covering it with large pictures . . . [and] never saw a cat without thinking of a tiger or a lizard without thinking of a dragon." He drew and doodled on everything he touched, as well as illustrating his own and his friends' literary efforts.

The major change in his artistic style occurred when Chesterton went to the Slade School of Art. There, despite his jovial protestations that he loafed the whole time, his technique showed the development of a more "commercial" craft. He began to use stylized tricks for the bend of an elbow or the sweep of a pair of natty trousers; he began to sketch in rough page designs, then inked in the main lines, and shaded the rest to give the drawing a sharper contrast for mechanical reproduction. This technical transition can be seen by comparing the tiny illustrations that curl about the margins of his schoolboy clerihews with the 1905 *Biography for Beginners*, in which his carefully composed full-page illustrations have strong key lines and a three-dimensional look is achieved with more practiced shading.

All his life, though, Chesterton doodled heads of Gladstone or Shaw or Napoleon in much the same way. His young admirer Nicholas Bentley reported that his chalk drawings were drawn free style, and said that it was watching Chesterton put a character like Cyrano de Bergerac or the Cid down on brown paper with clear deliberate strokes that gave him the idea that drawing was the easiest thing in the world to do.

Throughout his career, Chesterton the writer never ceased to be a visual artist. He worked as an illustrator and political cartoonist, as well as a "weekend painter" who entertained his friends with storybook drawings or toy theatre productions or treasure hunts. He was author and illustrator of his first published book, *Greybeards at Play*, which contained nonsense verse he had written to amuse a child. For this book Chesterton re-did his earlier drawings, creating half-page illustrations, like those about the wild-haired old philosopher with the enormous nose who sits besides an aged pig with an identical snout, or those illustrating "The Disastrous Spread of Aestheticism in All Classes," where one verse shows a tattered sky in which Chagall-like creatures stream past. That same year he also illustrated a book of nonsense verse by Cosmo Monkhouse.

From 1902 to 1909, Chesterton continued to draw political cartoons for *The Speaker*, illustrated satiric verse by Hilaire Belloc and articles by E. V. Lucas, re-illustrated their clerihews for Bentley's *Biography for Beginners*, and did his first set of 34 free-hand illustrations for a Belloc novel, *Emmanuel Burden*. He was to illustrate only one novel of his own, *The Club of Queer Trades*, but he continued to his life's end to contribute drawings to succeeding editions of Bentley's clerihews and draw the free-hand illustrations around which Belloc then wrote his novels, as well as to produce front-page cartoons for G. K.'s *Weekly* when needed. His artwork was a form of his general kindliness, for there is no evidence that he was ever paid for his work.

At the same time, his characteristic, incessant "doodling" was apparently a method of releasing his imagination so his ideas would flow. He described the process in *Tremendous Trifles* where, in the essay "A Piece of Chalk," Chesterton set out on the downs to sketch armed with his favorite brown paper and a pocketful of chalks. He did not plan to draw the countryside but

"the fertile dragons of his imagination." Once at work, he found he had no white chalk, which he had to have for "philosophizing" because the color white is not the absence of color but a "shining and affirmative thing." Suddenly he sat up and laughed at himself, for all the time he had been sitting on a great "warehouse of chalk," England. The essay not only leaves his reader with a vivid picture of Chesterton at work but also makes him aware of Chesterton's sadness that England is not visibly "white" anymore.

Paradoxically, the most important period for Chesterton's development as a writer was also the time he spent at the Slade School of Art. It "solidified" the direction of his thought and changed his choice of a profession. It was the period when he personally suffered the rigors of adolescent confusion and despair, but an equally important factor in his development was the situation he found at the Slade when he went there in 1892.

It was a time when, through the good offices of George Moore, who was to be

portrayed later as a great Chestertonian heretic, the Slade professors and the English public were being introduced to French Impressionism and the aesthetic principles of Walter Pater, which preached the disassociation of the visionary aesthetic moment from any moral or emotional framework. Translated into the Slade's teaching, however, "Impressionism" did not mean a loosening of technique but the very opposite, a strict, tense anxiety about the exact "tone" or "value," which created those serious, narrow-minded young specialists whom Chesterton refused to join in their frenzied attempt to "keep abreast of Whistler; to take him by the white forelock, as if he were time himself."

It was at the Slade, therefore, that Chesterton began his lifelong crusade against the immorality that said that "things only exist as we perceive them, or that things do not exist at all." As Chesterton whimsically put it, contrary to the everyday common sense of ordinary men, the artistic principle of Impressionism was that "if all that could be seen of a cow was a white line and a purple shadow, we should only render the line and the shadow; in a sense we should only believe in the line and the shadow, rather than in the cow."

Chesterton had grown up a debater, who defended his ideas in combat and, by parrying the views of his opponents, discovered his own. Just so, Chesterton the artist developed his very decided aesthetic in opposition to the Impressionists and the aesthetes. He demanded the "morality" of

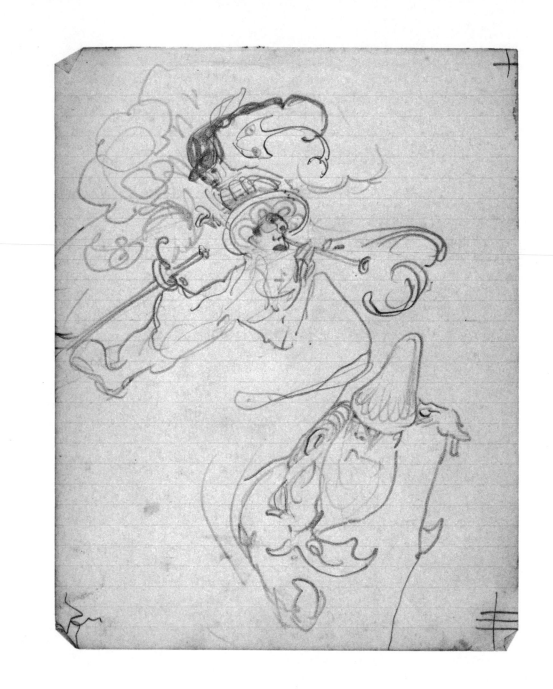

strong lines and sharp edges, the use of distinct and dramatic colors without any blurring or rubbing out of the outline. During his entire career he defended this aesthetic against the forces of relativism and skepticism. In his passionate identification with the ordinary man, he further insisted that man was made in the image of God as an artist, which was the role that separated him from the beasts. He made the point most dramatically in *The Everlasting Man* when he described what the priest and the boy found in the French caves: "drawings and paintings of animals ... not only by a man but by an artist ... that showed that love of the long sweeping or long wavering line which any man who has ever drawn will ... recognize." His ultimate philosophical purpose was to re-unite art and religion, for "all art is religious art ... and the public art of the people."

At the very same time he was tilting against art for art's sake, Chesterton in his writing remained and is remembered as "a fugitive from the *fin de siécle*." Chesterton's written work is redolent with Impressionistic images that remain with his reader. Time after time, in his writing, his most telling points are images or descriptions that make his point: Innocent Smith blows over the wall; or Chesterton the yachtsman, armed to the teeth, bravely plants the British flag at Brighton Pavilion; or a mob attacks a city lamp-post defended by a monk; or Colonel Crane eats his raw cabbage hat.

The many memorable landscapes in his

fiction are also cunningly and artistically crafted. They not only set the story's mood, but they themselves are dynamic, changing within a story to suggest deeper levels of meaning that work for a restoration of Chestertonian health and balance. A spectacular example is the Father Brown story "The Sins of Prince Saradine," in which the opening journey begins in a golden fairyland which then turns prosaic, ordinary colors, but becomes a furious red at the climax, only to fade away again into pale green and white. This visual description reflects the process of Flambeau's understanding of the crime.

Chesterton also wrote two full-length studies of artists in which he recapitulated his own artistic development. The first was G.F. *Watts*, a study of the Kensington artist who had painted the murals in Parliament and many portraits of the great Victorians from Alfred Lord Tennyson to Leslie Stephen, making them, Chesteron said, larger than life. Chesterton began by praising Watts because he regarded life as a whole, not separating art from ethics, and never accepted the theory that "art's affair was its own love of a great billowing line for its own sake." But then he pointed out that Watts's work corresponded closely to his "early Victorian puritanism," which took the form of a primordial "paganism" reflected in Watts' cold primeval dawns and red-earth women drawn in the clay colors of the Eternal Potter. Here Chesterton used an artistic figure of speech he was to return to again and again in his writing, saying that Watt's colors had a pagan opaqueness in

"A man from the American Embassy, who said nothing...."

The Hedge & the Horse.

which a light shines upon things, rather than the Christian transparency of a Botticelli in which light always shines through.

His second full-length study of an artist was *William Blake*, published in 1910. Chesterton began by saying that Blake's character was quite solid but quite queer, with his own kind of natural super-naturalism. Blake's training in classic engraving had taught him to be a fanatic on the firm line, which meant he was against "Impressionism"; being a mystic, though, Blake also drew his perfect figures "upside down," as he did in his design called "Space," where the Almighty, foreshortened in colossol perspective, bends forward to trace out the heavens with a compass. Chesterton saw Blake as a man of the eighteenth century, which ended in revolution because it began in law, an age of reason in which paganism rose again. Blake, he said, belonged in the company of mystics who exaggerate reality but do not distort it, and his final judgment on Blake was that "in the everlasting battle . . . Blake is on the side of the angels . . . and all sensible men, because Blake chose the better side in the duel between the artist who has the higher and harder ambition to be a man" and the narrow specialist.

In all his writing Chesterton used art for his analogies, again revealing that it was as an artist that he viewed the world. In *Orthodoxy*, for example, he explained that "art is limitation; the essence of every picture is the frame. If you draw a giraffe, you must draw him with a long neck. If, in your bold, creative way you . . . draw him with a short neck, you . . . will find you are not free to draw a giraffe."

Later in the same book he suggested that progress towards the New Jerusalem is endless because men keep changing the ideal instead of marching towards the real. The result is the same as if a man wanted to paint the world blue. If he worked at it steadily day by day he might accomplish it, but not if he started over each day to paint it a different color. Whistler may have done twenty studies to do a portrait, but he did not draw a new model twenty times.

For Chesterton, finally, the artist must be "in the core of the cosmos, not on its revolving edges, where there is no central stalk of sanity." That sanity and balance, which is Chesterton's gift to the world, he expressed once more in artistic terms in *Saint Thomas Aquinas* when he wrote that "the strangeness of things, which is the light in all poetry, and indeed in all art, is . . . their otherness . . . or their objectivity . . . The great contemplative is the complete contrary of that . . . selfish artist who . . . lives only in his own mind."

In the last analysis, the "art" of G. K. Chesterton was his gift, his genius, for getting at the heart of things and making "their objectivity" as plain as a pikestaff—in words or pictures. He seems to have taken it as his "vocation," almost as a crusade, to defend the objectivity of things and the soundness of common sense against "the lunatics" of relativism and of skepticism. One can almost see him living out, in a

somewhat turbulent lifetime, the image of that wild charioteer, truth, he described in *Orthodoxy*, thundering along and bowling over heresies right and left.

"If anyone wants to know my opinions about [whatever]," he wrote in the introduction to *Orthodoxy*, "Mr. G. S. Street has only to throw me another challenge, and I will write him another book." Just as he arrived for his debates with Shaw late, disheveled, and in haste, dripping notes on bits of paper, one imagines his true "genius" not to have been to paint (or write) great masterpieces but rather to "toss off" bits of paper—chalk sketches or cartoons, essays or poems, and, yes, even books—in defense of sanity and common sense, of those "tremendous trifles" at the heart of all things human and divine. He saw clearly, he drew clearly, he wrote clearly; but always with a point of view, a "perspective" that included the whole of creation and not just a part of the whole. And it was his defense of the common sense of the common man, rooted in eternal truths as a result of creation, that makes his "art" so ageless—and so badly needed again in our age.

Appendix

Major Works in Chronological Order

Note: The editions listed are the first editions. Since there is no uniform edition of Chesterton's works, anyone wishing more detailed information about editions must consult John Sullivan's G. K. Chesterton: A Bibliography (London: University of London Press, 1958) and its sequels.

1900: *Greybeards at Play*. London: R. Brimley Johnson.
The Wild Knight and Other Poems. London: Grant Richards.
1901: *The Defendent*. London: R. Brimley Johnson.
1902: *Twelve Types*. London: Arthur Humphreys.
1903: *Robert Browning*. London: Macmillan & Co.
1904: *G. F. Watts*. London: Duckworth & Co.
The Napoleon of Notting Hill. London: John Lane, The Bodley Head.
1905: *The Club of Queer Trades*. London: Harper Brothers.
Heretics. London: John Lane, The Bodley Head.
1906: *Charles Dickens*. London: Metheun & Co.

1908: *The Man Who Was Thursday.* Bristol: J. W. Arrowsmith.
All Things Considered. London: Metheun & Co.
Orthodoxy. London: John Lane, The Bodley Head.

1909: *George Bernard Shaw.* London: John Lane, The Bodley Head.
Tremendous Trifles. London: Metheun & Co.
The Ball and the Cross. London: Wells Gardner, Darton & Co.

1910: *What's Wrong With the World.* London: Cassell and Company.
Alarms and Discursions. London: Metheun & Co.
William Blake. London: Duckworth & Co.

1911: *Appreciations and Criticisms of the Works of Charles Dickens:* London: J. M. Dent & Sons
The Innocence of Father Brown. London: Cassell & Co.
The Ballad of the White Horse. London: Metheun & Co.

1912: *Manalive.* London: Thomas Nelson & Sons
A Miscellany of Men. London: Metheun & Co.

1913: *The Victorian Age in Literature.* London: Williams and Norgate.
Magic: A Fantastic Comedy. London: Martin Secker.

1914: *The Flying Inn.* London: Metheun & Co.
The Wisdom of Father Brown. London: Cassell & Co.

1915: *Poems.* London: Burns & Oates, Ltd.

1917: *A Short History of England.* London: Chatto & Windus.
Utopia of Usurers. New York: Boni & Liveright.

1919: *Irish Impressions.* London: W. Collins Sons & Co.

1920: *The Superstition of Divorce.* London: Chatto & Windus.
The Uses of Diversity. London: Metheun & Co.
The New Jerusalem. London: Hodder & Stoughton.

1922: *Eugenics and Other Evils.* London: Cassell & Co.
What I Saw in America. London: Hodder & Stoughton.
The Ballad of Saint Barbara. London: Cecil Palmer.
The Man Who Knew Too Much. London: Cassell & Co.

1923: *Fancies Versus Fads.* London: Metheun & Co.
St. Francis of Assisi. London: Hodder & Stoughton Ltd.

1925: *Tales of the Long Bow.* London: Cassell & Company.
The Everlasting Man. London: Hodder & Stoughton.
William Cobbett. London: Hodder & Stoughton.

1926: *The Incredulity of Father Brown.* London: Cassell & Co.
The Outline of Sanity. London: Metheun & Co.
The Queen of Seven Swords. London: Sheed & Ward.

1927:   *The Catholic Church and Conversion.* London: Burns, Oates, & Washbourne, Ltd.
        The Return of Don Quixote. London: Chatto & Windus.
        The Collected Poems of G. K. Chesterton. London: Cecil Palmer.
        The Secret of Father Brown. London: Cassell & Co.
        The Judgment of Dr. Johnson. London: Sheed & Ward.
        Robert Louis Stevenson. London: Hodder & Stoughton.
1928:   *Generally Speaking.* London: Metheun & Co.
1929:   *The Poet and the Lunatics.* London: Cassell & Co.
        The Thing: Why I Am A Catholic. London: Sheed & Ward.
        G.K.C. as M.C.. London: Metheun & Co.
1930:   *Four Faultless Felons.* London: Cassell & Co.
        The Resurrection of Rome. London: Hodder & Stoughton.
        Come to Think of It. London: Metheun & Co.
1931:   *All is Grist.* London: Metheun & Co.
1932:   *Chaucer.* London: Faber & Faber Ltd.
        Sidelights on New London and Newer York. London: Sheed & Ward.
1933:   *All I Survey.* London: Metheun & Co.
        St. Thomas Aquinas: the Dumb Ox. London: Hodder & Stoughton Ltd.
1934:   *Avowals and Denials.* London: Metheun & Co.
1935:   *The Scandal of Father Brown.* London: Cassell & Co.
        The Well and the Shallows. London: Sheed & Ward.
1936:   *As I Was Saying.* London: Metheun & Co.

Posthumous Books

1936: *Autobiography.* London: Hutchinson & Co.
1937: *The Paradoxes of Mr. Pond.* London: Cassell & Co.
1938: *The Coloured Lands.* London: Sheed & Ward.
1940: *The End of the Armistice.* London: Sheed & Ward.
1950: *The Common Man.* London: Sheed & Ward.
1952: *The Surprise.* London: Sheed & Ward.
1953: *A Handful of Authors.* London: Sheed & Ward.
1955: *The Glass Walking-Stick.* London: Metheun & Co.
1958: *Lunacy and Letters.* London: Sheed & Ward.
1964: *The Spice of Life.* Beaconsfield: Darwen Finlayson.

Chronological List of Books and Periodicals with Illustrations by G. K. Chesterton

1900: *The Speaker.* September and October, Front-page cartoons. *Greybeards at Play.* Rhymes and Sketches by Gilbert Chesterton. London: R. Brimley Johnson.

        Nonsense Rhymes. By Cosmo Monkhouse. Cover design and illustrations by Gilbert Chesterton.

1903: *The Great Inquiry.* Faithfully Reported by H.B. Reporter and Ornamented with Sharp Cuts Drawn on the Spot by G.K.C. London: Duckworth.

        The Speaker. December 12. Two illustrations to *An Annual Problem. Books for Children.* by E.V. Lucas. Three illustrations to *What A Child Wants* by Hilaire Belloc.

1904: *The Idler.* June to December. Illustrations to the serialized version of *The Club of Queer Trades.*

        Emmanuel Burden. By Hilaire Belloc, with 34 illustrations by G.K. Chesterton. London: Metheun & Co.

        The Speaker. December 10. Seven Illustrations to *Children's Books,* by E.V. Lucas.

1905: *The Club of Queer Trades.*

        Biography for Beginners. Being a Collection of Miscellaneous Examples for the use of Upper Forms. Edited by E. Clerihew, B.A. With 40 Diagrams by G.K. Chesterton. London: T. Werner Laurie. Reprinted in *Clerihews Complete.* London: Metheun & Co. 1951; *The Complete Clerihews of* E. Clerihew Bentley. Oxford: Oxford University Press, 1981;

The First Clerihews by E. Clerihew Bentley & Collaborators. Illustrated by G.K. Chesterton. Oxford: Oxford University Press, 1982.

The Speaker. December 9. Five illustrations to *On Children's Books* by Hilaire Belloc.

1909: *Fairy Tales from the German Forests.* By Frau Arndt. London: Everett. Colored Frontispiece: The Dwarf and colored title page by G.K. Chesterton.

Granta. December. A drawing "After the Bump Supper."

1911: *Strand Magazine.* April. Drawing of "Dons Disproving the Sea Serpent."

The Odd Volume. Edited by John O. Wilson. Four drawings of "Villains Plotting, Mr. Pecksniff and Rashleigh Osbaldistone, Count Fosco and Mr. Quilp, The Master of Ballantrae and Bill Sykes: Eugenics."

1912: *The Green Overcoat.* By Hilaire Belloc with Illustrations by G.K. Chesterton

1914: *The British Review.* August. Illustrations to "Eccles of Beccles" by Wilfred Ward.

1922: *The Mercy of Allah.* By Hilaire Belloc. Drawing on dust jacket by G. K. Chesterton.

1924: *Stampede!* by L. de Giberne Sieveking. Frontispiece and illustrations by G. K. Chesterton.

1925: *Mr. Petrie.* By Hilaire Belloc. 22 Drawings by G. K. Chesterton.

G.K.'s Weekly. December 5. 2 illustrations for "The Turkey and the Turk", one illustration for *The Return of Don Quixote.*

1926: *The Emerald.* By Hilaire Belloc. 22 drawings by G.K. Chesterton.

G.K.'s Weekly. February 27. "A Biography for Beginners." March 6. "Another Biography for Beginners." March 13. "A Third Biography for Beginners." March 20. "A Fourth Biography for Beginners." March 27. "A Fifth Biography for Beginners."

1927: *The Haunted House.* By Hilaire Belloc. 25 illustrations by G.K. Chesterton.

1928: *But Soft—We are Observed.* By Hilaire Belloc. 25 illustrations by G.K. Chesterton.

1929: *More Biography.* By E. Clerihew Bentley. G.K.C. contributed 15 drawings which appeared in *Pall Mall Magazine* May-September.

The Missing Masterpiece. By Hilaire Belloc. 41 illustrations by G.K. Chesterton.

1930: *The Man Who Made Gold.* By Hilaire Belloc. 17 drawings by G.K. Chesterton.

G.K.'s Weekly. December 27. G.K.C. cartoon: "The Merger."

1931: *G.K.'s Weekly.* January 10. G.K.C. cartoon "On an American Best-Seller."

Mutt's Mutterings 1931. G.K.C. cartoon "By one who might be a Mutt, but prefers to be a Mug."

1932: *The Postmaster-General.* By Hilaire Belloc. 30 drawings by G.K. Chesterton.

Reading, Writing, and Remembering. by E.V. Lucas. Reprints two *Speaker* illustrations and sketch "Sacred to the Memory of E.V. Lucas."

G.K.'s Weekly. December 10. Front-page cartoon.

1933: *Pauline and Old Pauline.* By H.A. Sams. 2 G.K.C. drawings.

1934:   G.K.'s *Weekly.* October 11. G.K.C. cartoon.
            G.K.'s *Weekly.* December 13. Front-page cartoon.
1935:   G.K.'s *Weekly.* March 21. Tenth Birthday Number. Cartoon.
            G.K.'s *Weekly.* July 11. Front-page cartoon.
            G.K.'s *Weekly.* October 10. Front-page cartoon.
            G.K.'s *Weekly.* October 17. Front-page cartoon.
            G.K.'s *Weekly.* November 7. Front-page cartoon.
1936:   *The Hedge and the Horse.* By Hilaire Belloc. 40 illustrations by G.K. Chesterton.

Major Posthumous Publication of G.K.C. Art

1938: *The Coloured Lands*.

1941: *As It Hapened*. An Autobiography by Maurice B. Reckitt. A page of G.K.C. doodles.

1944: *Gilbert Keith Chesterton*. By Maisie Ward. Early self-caricature and two pages of toy theatre puppets.

1952: *Return to Chesterton*. By Maisie Ward. 6 pages of drawings.
Catholic Herald. December 5. 11 illustrations to "A vision of Edens."
Catholic Herald. December 26. A page of unpublished drawings "From the Cradle to the Grave."

1953: *The Saturday Book*. Edited by John Hadfield. G.K.C. Thank-you poem and cartoon sent to Mrs. Masterman, "Lo! Masterman and Chesterton."

1957: *The Listener*. January 3. Cartoon "The Viking and the Very Tame Lion."
The Eye of the Beholder. By Lance Sieveking. 3 Drawings: "Mr. Chesterton discovers he is twenty years late for school" (drawn for L. Sieveking in 1912), illustration from *Stampede*, and "The Viking and the Very Tame Lion," originally drawn in L. Sieveking's copy of *A Miscellany of Men*.

1964: *Theatre Notebook*. Summer. "Hiram Stead and Sir Henry Irving" by G.K. Chesterton.

1974: G.K. *Chesterton, A Centenary Appraisal*. Edited by John Sullivan. Drawing of Christ by G.K.C. at age 7, page of nonsense verse with marginal illustrations (1898), cover for first edition of *Greybeards at Play*, pen and ink drawing of "Captain Poker, Rev. Ezra Plumtree, and Professor Splosch" (1893), cartoon "First Impressions of Beaconsfield & My dog" (1909), Masterman Thank-you poem and cartoon, puppets from the toy theatre, illustration from Hilaire Belloc's *The Missing Masterpiece*.

G.K. *Chesterton 1874-1936. A Centenary Exhibition*. May 14-31. National Book League. Arranged by John Sullivan. (Catalogue). Illustrations reproduced in catalogue: drawing, aged 7; puppets from toy theatre; manuscript of "Lepanto."

Gilbert Keith Chesterton. An Exhibition Catalogue of English and American First Editions on the Occasion of the Centenary of His Birth. Wahlert Memorial Library, Loras College, Dubuque, Iowa. Catalogue illustrations include: cartoon "The Defendant" inscription in Belloc's copy; Frontis-page G.K.'s *Weekly* Vol. 1, Number 1; illustration from "The disastrous spread of aestheticism in all classes"; manuscript poem to Thomas Hutchinson; illustration for "Lord Clive" from *Biography for Beginners*; illustration for "George the Third" from *More Biography*.

1983: *The Outline of Sanity. A Biography of G.K. Chesterton*. By Alzina Stone Dale. Illustrations by G.K.C. include: cartoon "I am late for my funeral" from series G.K.C.'s Famous After X-mas Cards; cartoon of "Edgar Allen Poe"; cartoon "Eugenics"; cartoons drawn for Notre Dame University's *Juggler*," Just Indignation of Queen Victoria" and "A true Victorian."

Index

Index

Index

DEMCO